Multi-vitamins for the Spirit: Anci
Spiritual, & Magical Good Luck
Love, Health, Money & Happines

The Ultimate All in One Guide to Get Good Luck!

How to Make Good Luck, Prayers for Good Luck, Spells for Good Luck, Feng Shui for Good Luck, and Good Luck Charms: More than 500 Ways to be Lucky in Love, Health, and Money

By Michael Junem

Dedicated to Humanity:
May this book bring you Good Energy like Benjamin Franklin brought us Electricity.

The Ultimate All in One Guide to Get Good Luck!

How to Make Good Luck, Prayers for Good Luck, Spells for Good Luck, Feng Shui for Good Luck, and Good Luck Charms: More than 500 Ways to be Lucky in Love, Health, and Money

All Rights Reserved © 2013 by
2 Heavens Productions at Createspace
ISBN 978-1482550313

Manufactured in the United States of America

No part of this book may be reproduced or transmitted in any form or by any means, graphic, electronic, or mechanical, including photocopying, recording, taping, or by any information storage retrieval system, without the permission in writing from the publisher.

2 Heavens Productions

http://www.2Heavens.com

Publisher's Cataloging in Publication

Junem, Michael
The Ultimate All in One Guide to Get Good Luck!

How to Make Good Luck, Prayers for Good Luck, Spells for Good Luck, Feng Shui for Good Luck, and Good Luck Charms: More than 500 Ways to be Lucky in Love, Health, and Money [Michael Junem]
1st ed. P. Cm.
Includes bibliographical references.

Table of Contents

INTRODUCTION..17
   THE FIVE PILLARS OF GOOD LUCK...17
   TOTAL GOOD LUCK...17
   LUCK IS ENERGY..18
   OPEN ENERGY...20

MAKE GOOD LUCK..24
   1.   *Frequency of Trying*..*24*
   2.   *Do not hide from luck*...*24*
   3.   *Staying cool for luck*...*25*
   4.   *Experience luck*..*25*
   5.   *Exercise luck*..*25*
   6.   *Listen to luck*..*26*
   7.   *Expect good luck*..*27*
   8.   *Make Luck your Goal*..*28*
   9.   *See Good Luck*..*28*

GOOD LUCK IN LOVE..30
   CHINESE GOOD LUCK IN LOVE 30
   10.   *Good Feng shui to enhance your love life:*..................*30*
   11.   *Feng shui to prevent love*...*30*
   12.   *Feng shui To Protect love*...*30*
   13.   *Feng shui to attract love*..*31*
   14.   *Feng shui to attract love*..*31*
   15.   *Feng shui to attract love*..*31*
   16.   *Feng shui to attract love*..*32*
   17.   *Feng shui to attract love*..*32*
   18.   *Feng shui to attract love*..*32*
   19.   *Feng shui to prevent love*...*33*
   20.   *Feng shui to prevent love*...*33*
   21.   *Feng shui to prevent love*...*33*
   22.   *Feng shui to prevent love*...*33*
   23.   *Feng shui to prevent love*...*34*
   24.   *Feng shui to prevent love*...*34*
   WICCAN GOOD LUCK IN LOVE 34
   25.   *Magic spell for More Joy and Love*.............................*34*
   26.   *Magic spell for Anti-loneliness*....................................*35*
   27.   *Magic spell for letting go of a past love*....................*36*
   28.   *Magic spell for Love Attraction*..................................*37*
   29.   *Magic spell for The Heart Healing* *38*
   JEWISH GOOD LUCK IN LOVE 39
   30.   *Prayer to mend a broken heart*..................................*39*

31. Prayer for an easy end to a romance 39
32. Prayer to find forgiveness 39
33. Prayer to find True and lasting love 39
34. Prayer to open the eyes of those who will not see 39
35. Prayer to protect a loved one 40
36. Prayer to have your partner be a better lover 40
37. Prayer to be a better lover 40
38. Prayer to stop someone from stealing your lover 40
39. Prayer to turn an enemy into a friend 41
40. Prayer to Make someone dream of you 41
41. Prayer for reconciliation 41
42. Prayer to gain forgiveness 41
43. Prayer to rid yourself of a bothersome lover 42
44. Prayer for new love and romance 42
45. Prayer against Betrayal: - 42
46. Prayer for Marriage Blessings: - 42
47. Prayer to reclaim lost destiny: - 42
48. Prayer for the Unity of all Nations: - 43
49. Prayer of Confidence: - 43
50. Prayer for a Successful Marriage: - 43

CHRISTIAN GOOD LUCK IN LOVE 43
51. Prayer For new love and romance 43
52. Prayer against loneliness 44
53. Prayer to impart kindness in a cold heart 44
54. Prayer to find a better lover 44
55. Prayer to rekindle the fire in a romance 44
56. Prayer to stop a lover from cheating 45
57. Prayer to End an argument 45
58. Prayer to bring back a lost lover 45
59. Prayer to gain trust and favor 45
60. Prayer for Protection of Widows: - 46
61. Prayer for Faithfulness: - 46
62. Prayer for the Entire World: - 46
63. Prayer of Confidence: 46

MUSLIM GOOD LUCK IN LOVE 46
64. Prayer For love (Wife & Husband) 47
65. Prayer for love (Wife & Husband) 47
66. Prayer For love (Wife & Husband) 47
67. Prayer for Light in your Heart 47
68. Prayer for Steadfastness of the heart 48
69. Prayer for a Spouse 48
70. Prayer for love 49
71. Prayer to find a spouse 49
72. Prayer for a spouse 49

73.	Prayer for Parents	49
74.	Prayer for Parents	50
75.	Prayer for Parents	50
76.	Prayer For parents	50
77.	Prayer For the return of someone who has absconded	50
78.	Prayer for children	50
79.	Prayer for Piety in the family	51
80.	Prayer for removing suspicion and doubt	51
81.	Prayer to get married	51
82.	Prayer for mercy on family	59
83.	Prayer for mercy on family	60
84.	Prayer by Children for Parents	60

GOOD LUCK CHARMS IN LOVE ... 60

85.	A Key	60
86.	A Heart	61
87.	Munachi Amulet	61
88.	Norse sigil,	61
89.	Loving Friends Incense	62
90.	Attract a Lover Incense t	62
91.	Attract Love Incense	62
92.	To Attract Love:	62
93.	Attracting men:	63
94.	Pink candle	63
95.	Love stones.	63
96.	Feldspar	63
97.	Morganite	64
98.	Sardonyx	64
99.	Azurite	64
100.	Emerald	64

MANIFEST GOOD LUCK IN LOVE ... 64

101.	Manifest the image	64
102.	Manifest the details	65
103.	Manifest the words	65
104.	Manifest love in yourself	65

GOOD LUCK IN HEALTH ... **67**

CHINESE GOOD LUCK IN HEALTH ... 67

105.	Feng shui To improve your health,	67
106.	Feng shui that prevents health,	67
107.	Feng shui to Enhance the Health Sector	67
108.	Feng shui color for health	67
109.	Feng shui shapes for health	68
110.	Feng shui pictures for health	68
111.	Feng shui fruit for health	68

112.	Feng shui symbols for health	68
113.	Feng shui humor for health	69
114.	Feng shui that prevents health	69
115.	Feng shui that prevents health	69
116.	Feng shui that prevents health	69
117.	Feng Shui for Fertility	70
118.	Feng Shui for Fertility	70
119.	Feng Shui for Fertility	70
120.	Feng Shui for Fertility	70
121.	Feng Shui for Fertility	70
122.	Feng Shui for Fertility	71

WICCAN GOOD LUCK IN HEALTH 71

123.	Spell for Improving Vision, Clarity, Eyesight	71
124.	Spell for Improving Hearing, Improving Clairaudience	71
125.	Spell for Even Flow	72
126.	Spell For Soothing A Stress Headache	72
127.	A Spell To Make Anything Healing	72
128.	Spell Against A Person Who Wishes You Harm	73
129.	Spell for Healing	73
130.	Spell against stress	73

JEWISH GOOD LUCK IN HEALTH 74

131.	Prayer To banish all that would do harm to you or any loved	74
132.	Prayer For protection in time of war	74
133.	Prayer For fertility	74
134.	Prayer To have a trouble free night of sleep	75
135.	Prayer Always awaken fresh and full of energy	75
136.	Prayer Enhance your powers physically and mentally	75
137.	Prayer To overcome a strong enemy	75
138.	Prayer Protection while traveling	76
139.	Prayer To attract good health	76
140.	Prayer to heal disease associated with old age	76
141.	Prayer to heal depression and anxiety	76
142.	Prayer to stop bleeding	77
143.	Prayer against the spread of venereal diseases: -	77
144.	Prayer Against Natural Disasters -	77
145.	Prayer Against Fire outbreak: -	77
146.	Prayer for Little Children: -	77
147.	Prayer for Little Children: -	78
148.	Prayer for Safe Delivery of Pregnant Woman:	78
149.	Prayer Against Boat Mishap, Air crash and Road Accident: -	78
150.	Prayer to fight every form of Social ills/vices in our Society: -	78
151.	Prayer to fight every form of Social ills/vices in our Society: -	79
152.	Prayer for Quick Recovery from Sickness/Infirmity: -	79
153.	Prayer Against Spiritual Loss: -	79

154.	Prayer for Protection: -	79
155.	Prayer to End Violence: -	79
156.	Prayer to End Violence: -	80
157.	Prayer for Good Health: -	80
158.	Prayer Against Bad Luck:	80
159.	Prayer for Long life: -	80
160.	Prayer Against Miscarriage: -	81
161.	Prayer against Untimely Death: -	81
162.	Prayer for Success in Examinations: -	81
163.	Prayer to have babies (boys/girls): -	81
164.	Prayer for fruit of the womb: -	81
165.	Prayer for fruit of the womb: -	82

CHRISTIAN GOOD LUCK IN HEALTH 82

166.	Prayer To heal any sickness	82
167.	Prayer to send healing energies to someone	82
168.	Prayer to Contact your guardian angel	82
169.	Prayer To send away bad health	82
170.	Prayer to Heal from injuries and chronic pain	83
171.	Prayer to Heal from warts and other growths	83
172.	Prayer to heal for any kind of sickness	83
173.	Prayer for healing high blood pressure	83
174.	Prayer for healing from infections	84
175.	Prayer for Healing cold, flu and lung problems	84
176.	Prayer for healing alcoholism	84
177.	Prayer for healing stomach and eating disorders	84
178.	Prayer for Safe Delivery of Pregnant Woman: -	85
179.	Prayer to be strengthened in fasting	85
180.	Prayer to be strengthened in fasting	85
181.	Prayer for Quick Recovery from Sickness/Infirmity: -	85
182.	Prayer Against Bad Luck:	86
183.	Prayer to break barrenness: -	86
184.	Prayer to heal sickness/diseases: -	86

MUSLIM GOOD LUCK IN HEALTH 86

185.	Prayer For increase of breast milk	86
186.	Prayer for any sickness	87
187.	Prayer for any sickness	87
188.	Prayer for any sickness	87
189.	Prayer for any sickness	87
190.	Prayer for any sickness	87
191.	Prayer for Fever	87
192.	Prayer for Fever	88
193.	Prayer for security against all harms	88
194.	Prayer for security against all harms	88
195.	Prayer for security against all harms	88

196.	Prayer for security against all harms	89
197.	Prayer for security against all harms	89
198.	Prayer for security against all harms	89
199.	Prayer for security against all harms	89
200.	Prayer for security against all harms	89
201.	Prayer for protecting children against infantile diseases	90
202.	Prayer for healthy upbringing of children	90
203.	Prayer for Seeking Health	90
204.	Prayer for Seeking health	90
205.	Prayer for Seeking protection	91
206.	Prayer for Seeking protection	91
207.	Prayer for Seeking Protection	91
208.	Prayer for General Well Being	91
209.	Prayer for general well being	92
210.	Prayer for general well being	92
211.	Prayer for General well being	92
212.	Prayer for When fearing an attack from an animal	93
213.	Prayer to prevent entering the house	93
214.	Prayer to protect against snakes	93
215.	Prayer to protection against animals	93
216.	Prayer for Insomnia	94
217.	Prayer for Bone fracture	94
218.	Prayer for Itching of the body	94
219.	Prayer for Inflammation of the eyes	94
220.	Prayer for Strengthening the eyesight	95
221.	Prayer for Headaches	95
222.	Prayer For a specific pain	95
223.	Prayer for Disease of the spleen	95
224.	Prayer for palpitation of the heart	95
225.	Prayer for protection of a vessel	96
226.	Prayer for When the seas are rough	96
227.	Prayer for Improving the memory	96
228.	Prayer for safety in travelling	96
229.	Prayer for mercy and removal of difficulties.	97
230.	Prayer for mercy on family	97
231.	Prayer for mercy and removal of difficulties.	97
232.	Prayer for protection during war	97
233.	Prayer for protection during war	97
234.	Prayer for protection during war	98
235.	Prayer for protection during war	98
236.	Prayer for regaining health	98
237.	Prayer for safety.	98
GOOD LUCK CHARMS IN HEALTH		98
238.	A Wheel	98

239.	A circle	99
240.	A Triangle	99
241.	A Crescent	99
242.	A Sapphire	100
243.	Lucky bamboo	100
244.	Turtles	101
245.	Tortoises	101
246.	Dolphins	101
247.	Eggs	101
248.	A Cricket	102
249.	Healing Incense	102
250.	Healing Incense	102
251.	Healing Incense	103
252.	Regain Health Incense	103
253.	For Healing:	103
254.	For Fertility:	103
255.	Green candle	104
256.	Agate	104
257.	Aventurine	104
258.	Jade	104
259.	Sapphire	105
260.	Tiger's eye	105

MANIFEST GOOD LUCK IN HEALTH 105

| 261. | Manifest laughter | 105 |
| 262. | Manifest a perfect body | 106 |

GOOD LUCK IN WEALTH 107

CHINESE GOOD LUCK IN WEALTH 107

263.	Feng shui to attract fame	107
264.	Feng shui that prevents wealth	107
265.	Feng shui to attract wealth	107
266.	Feng shui to attract wealth	108
267.	Feng shui to attract wealth	108
268.	Feng shui that prevents wealth	108
269.	Feng shui that prevents a Good Reputation	109
270.	Feng shui that prevents a Good Reputation	109
271.	Feng shui that attracts Opportunity	109
272.	Feng shui that attracts Opportunity	109
273.	Feng shui that attracts Opportunity	110
274.	Feng shui that attracts Opportunity	110
275.	Feng shui that attracts wealth	110
276.	Feng shui that attracts wealth	110
277.	Feng shui that attracts wealth	111
278.	Feng shui that attracts wealth	111

279.	Feng shui that attracts wealth	111
280.	Feng shui that prevents wealth	111
281.	Feng shui that prevents wealth	112
282.	Feng shui that prevents wealth	112

WICCAN GOOD LUCK IN WEALTH 112

283.	Money Energy Spell	112
284.	Spell for Understanding Money	113
285.	Spell for attracting money	113
286.	Spell for attracting wealth	114

JEWISH GOOD LUCK IN WEALTH 115

287.	Prayer To find lost money	115
288.	Prayer That debts will be repayed	115
289.	Prayer For luck with the lottery	116
290.	Prayer To attract wealth	116
291.	Prayer For success in making money	116
292.	Prayer To protect your home from fire	116
293.	Prayer for Favors from important people	117
294.	Prayer To stop thieves	117
295.	Prayer for Success from unfair competition	117
296.	Prayer to rise above any competition	117
297.	Prayer to Get better work from employees	117
298.	Prayer to Rid yourself of troubles with money or business	118
299.	Prayer For success in business	118
300.	Prayer for Good fortune in business and money	118
301.	Prayer for the Rich and Poor: -	118
302.	Prayer for the Rich and Poor: -	119
303.	Prayer for Economic Growth: -	119
304.	Prayer Against Economic woes: -	119
305.	Prayer against Promise and Fail: -	119
306.	Prayer for Success: -	119
307.	Prayer for Good Fortune: -	120
308.	Prayer for Positive Planning:	120
309.	Prayer Against Disappointments: -	120
310.	Prayer Against Rise and Fall: -	120
311.	Prayer for Wealth: -	120
312.	Prayer Against Poverty: -	120
313.	Prayer to Recover Lost Blessings: -	121
314.	Prayer for Promotion: -	121
315.	Prayer for Favor: -	121
316.	Prayer against blackmail by enemies:	121
317.	Prayer for Success in life's activities: -	122
318.	Prayer for Employment: -	122
319.	Prayer for Business opportunities: -	122

CHRISTIAN GOOD LUCK IN WEALTH 122

320.	Prayer To never have money worries again	122
321.	Prayer To get a raise	123
322.	Prayer To attract customers	123
323.	Prayer To get a better job	123
324.	Prayer for extra money	123
325.	Prayer for Breakthrough (Open doors): -	124
326.	Prayer for Divine Help/Wisdom: -	124
327.	Prayer against faulty foundation: -	124

MUSLIM GOOD LUCK IN WEALTH 124

328.	Prayer to find a lost object	124
329.	Prayer for Success in business	124
330.	Prayer for Success in business	125
331.	Prayer To increase sustenance	125
332.	Prayer For abundance	126
333.	Prayer For abundance	126
334.	Prayer to remove poverty	126
335.	Prayer to increase wealth	128
336.	Prayer for Repayment of debts	129
337.	Prayer for Wealth	129
338.	Prayer For protection against thieves	129
339.	Prayer for Blessings in business, farming, home, etc.	130
340.	Prayer for blessings in produce, livestock, etc	130
341.	Prayer For abundance in fortune	131
342.	Prayer For abundance in fortune	131
343.	Prayer for Repayment of debts	131

GOOD LUCK CHARMS IN WEALTH 132

344.	A Horn	132
345.	A Circle	132
346.	An Axe	132
347.	Coins	133
348.	Frogs	134
349.	Tigers	134
350.	Rainbows	134
351.	Alfalfa:	134
352.	Alkanet Root Bark:	135
353.	Alligator Tooth:	135
354.	Allspice Berries:	135
355.	Bayberry Root:	135
356.	Chamomile Hand Wash:	135
357.	Cinnamon Chips:	135
358.	Four-Leaf Clover:	135
359.	Horseshoe:	136
360.	John the Conquer Root:	136
361.	Lodestone:	136

- 362. Pyrite: 136
- 363. Rabbit Foot: 136
- 364. Silver Dime: 136
- 365. Money Incense 136
- 366. Orange candles 137
- 367. Crystals 137
- 368. Zircon 137
- 369. Chalcedony 137
- 370. Onyx 138
- 371. Almandine 138
- 372. Cat's eye 138
- 373. Blue John 138
- 374. Alunite 138

MANIFEST GOOD LUCK IN WEALTH 139
- 375. Manifest goals 139
- 376. Manifest money 139

GOOD LUCK IN HAPPINESS 140

CHINESE GOOD LUCK IN HAPPINESS 140
- 377. Feng shui to increase happiness 140
- 378. Feng shui to increase happiness 140
- 379. Feng shui to increase happiness 140
- 380. Feng shui that prevents happiness 140
- 381. Feng shui that prevents happiness 141
- 382. Feng shui that prevents happiness 141

WICCAN GOOD LUCK IN HAPPINESS 141
- 383. Spell For More Energy 141
- 384. Spell for "drawing out" curses and hexes from your energy 142

JEWISH GOOD LUCK IN HAPPINESS 143
- 385. Prayer to turn bad luck into good 143
- 386. Prayer To receive guidance 143
- 387. Prayer For good luck and happiness 144
- 388. Prayer To receive instructions in dreams 144
- 389. Prayer to remove any curse 144
- 390. Prayer To appreciate life to its fullest 144
- 391. Prayer To be free of unclean thoughts and deeds ...145
- 392. Prayer To find inner strength 145
- 393. Prayer To know the truth 145
- 394. Prayer to Cleanse the spirit 145
- 395. Prayer To turn sadness into joy 146
- 396. Prayer To dispel fear 146
- 397. Prayer To bring joy and happiness to your family 146
- 398. Prayer To gain prospective in the face of difficulty ...146
- 399. Prayer for Protection from malevolent spirits ...147

13

400.	Prayer To have a night of pleasant dreams	147
401.	Prayer Stop your boss from bothering you	147
402.	Prayer To receive an answer to a question	147
403.	Prayer to Remove bad luck and all curses	148
404.	Prayer To lose your troubles	148
405.	Prayer to gain spiritual power	148
406.	Prayer Make good wishes come true	148
407.	Prayer for the Good upbringing of Little Children: -	149
408.	Prayer for Courage and Patience: -	149
409.	Prayer Against War: -	149
410.	Prayer Against foul spirits/evil yoke: -	149
411.	Prayer for Continuous Growth and Up-liftment: -	149
412.	Prayer for Continuous Growth and Up-liftment: -	150
413.	Prayer Against Devilish Plans/water spirits:	150
414.	Prayer Against Devilish Plans/water spirits:	150
415.	Prayer for Peace, Oneness and Unity: -,	150
416.	Prayer for Peace, Oneness and Unity: -,	150
417.	Prayer Against Evil Initiations: -	151
418.	Prayer Against witches and wizards: -	151
419.	Prayer Against Monitoring spirits: -	151
420.	Prayer Against Occult Covenant:	151
421.	Prayer Against Evil curses: -	152

CHRISTIAN GOOD LUCK IN HAPPINESS 152

422.	Prayer To banish evil spirits	152
423.	Prayer To increase psychic powers	152
424.	Prayer Calm a troubled youth	152
425.	Prayer to Contact your spirit guide	153
426.	Prayer To rid yourself of bad dreams	153
427.	Prayer For wisdom and knowledge	153
428.	Prayer to Rid home of troublesome spirits	153
429.	Prayer to Cleanse a home from negative energy	153
430.	Prayer to Help a friend who is depressed	154
431.	Prayer To remove the evil eye	154
432.	Prayer to Remove a curse	154
433.	Prayer for good luck	154
434.	Prayer to Control Anger: -	155
435.	Prayer for good behavior: -	155
436.	Prayer Against Agents and rulers of darkness: -	155
437.	Prayer against Occult Serpent: -	155
438.	Prayer to Overcome the Devil:	155
439.	Prayer to Overcome the Devil:	156
440.	Prayer to defeat my enemies: -	156
441.	Prayer for Continuous Growth and Up-liftment: -	156
442.	Prayer for Religious Harmony: -	156

443.	Prayer for Peace, Oneness and Unity:	156
444.	Prayer to cast out evil spirits: -	157
445.	Prayer against Ancestral demons: -	157
446.	Prayer against forces of darkness: -	157

MUSLIM GOOD LUCK IN HAPPINESS 157

447.	Prayer for renewal of faith	157
448.	Prayer to strengthen your faith	157
449.	Prayer for melancholy and depression	158
450.	Prayer For melancholy and depression	158
451.	Prayer for Curing someone who is under the influence of evil	158
452.	Prayer for Curing someone who is under the influence of evil	158
453.	Prayer for curing someone who is under the influence of evil	159
454.	Prayer To remove fear and fright	159
455.	Prayer for Removing fear	160
456.	Prayer for Protection against evil men and jinn	160
457.	Prayer for protection against evil men and jinn	160
458.	Prayer for being In Distress	160
459.	Prayer for being In Distress	161
460.	Prayer for being In Distress	161
461.	Prayer for being In Distress	161
462.	Prayer for being in Distress	161
463.	Prayer for being In Distress	161
464.	Prayer for being In Distress	162
465.	Prayer for being In Distress	162
466.	Prayer for Protection from Satan	162
467.	Prayer for release from imprisonment	162
468.	Prayer for Nightmares	162
469.	Prayer For melancholy and depression	163
470.	Prayer For melancholy and depression	163
471.	Prayer For lessening one's burden	163
472.	Prayer for Curing someone under the influence of evil	163
473.	Prayer for Curing someone under the influence of evil	163
474.	Prayer to remove fear and fright	164
475.	Prayer for removing fear	164
476.	Prayer To halt an oppressor from oppressing	164
	Prayer for Removing of a calamity	164
477.	Prayer for divine help when trying to prove one's innocence.	165
478.	Prayer for gratitude	165

GOOD LUCK CHARMS FOR HAPPINESS 165

479.	Hand	165
480.	Cat's Eye	165
481.	Amber	166
482.	Nautical Star	166
483.	Horseshoe	166

484.	Red Chinese Lanterns	167
485.	Dream Catchers	167
486.	Red Bats	167
487.	Eggs	167
488.	Ladybugs	168
489.	Dragonflies	168
490.	Scarabs	169
491.	Improve Luck Incense	169
492.	Ending Negativity Incense	169
493.	Banishing evil Incense	169
494.	Jinx-removing Incense	170
495.	Exorcism Incense	170
496.	Luck:	170
497.	Happiness:	170
498.	Blue candle	170
499.	Aventurine	171
500.	Zircon	171
501.	Gypsum	171
502.	Pumice	171
503.	Rock crystal	172
504.	Chrysoprase	172
505.	Aquamarine	172
506.	Coral	172
507.	Carnelian	172

MANIFEST GOOD LUCK IN HAPPINESS 172
508.	Manifest your happiness	173
509.	Exercise the happiness	173

CONCLUSION **174**

Philosophy of Good Luck *174*
BIBLIOGRAPHY 177

Introduction

The Five Pillars of Good Luck

Like Islam, Good Luck has 5 pillars: physical powers (Making Good Luck), Balancing powers (Feng Shui), Earth powers (Spells and Charms), Spiritual powers (Prayers), and Mental powers (Manifestations).

Total Good Luck

Humans have **4 major healths**: physical, mental, financial and spiritual. Each of the 5 pillars of good luck are categorized and detailed for each of the 4 major healths, listing more than 500 ways to get good luck for your major healths.

The good luck pillars listed here have brought millions of people contentment and tranquility. Here is a brief description of each:

Making Good Luck: A study of over 1,000 people who consider themselves lucky and unlucky was made and the research of how their lifestyle increased their good luck is identified.

Chinese Feng Shui: Ancient Asian belief system based mainly on increasing good energy via the placement of certain objects in relation to certain elements. The belief system is similar to a computer circuit board where certain components made of various elements are placed in a particular pattern to create a desired flow of energy.

Wiccan Earth Magic: Nature based belief system using crystals, candles, herbs and incense to summon energy. Wiccans are diverse and differ in their belief system, for example, there are Christian Wiccans who only use their Lord to summon magic.

Jewish Bible: The Holy Book of Judaism, the first Abrahamic religion, Monotheists who believe in all the Prophets prior to Jesus.

Christian Gospel: The Holy Book of Christianity, the second Abrahamic religion, who believe in the Messiah Jesus is predicted in the Jewish Bible

Muslim Quran: The Holy Book of Islam, the third Abrahamic religion who believes Prophet Muhammad is predicted in the Jewish Bible and Christian Gospel, Islam is also the fastest growing religion.

Charms: Various earth items believed through history to attract certain energies, similar to plutonium emitting radiation, certain crystals, amulets, and symbols are also believed to emit certain energies.

Manifestation: The art of visualization and materializing good energy via a combination of belief systems.

Luck is Energy

Capturing and increasing unseen mysterious powers happens everyday, for example, splitting an unseen atom to create nuclear energy, reflecting the unseen rays of the sun to create solar energy, resisting the flow of unseen air to create wind energy.

Scientists spend billions and decades to research the unseen in nature and the universe, formulating methods of extracting good energy from various elements and forces in this world and beyond. The scientists use written formulas for capturing these unseen powers and converting them into good energy.

This book is a collection of written formulas used by **spiritual scientists** to capture good energy into your life to benefit you and your loved ones. These particular scientists have been called many things through time: Monks, Prophets, Witches, Wizards, and Shamans. The good energy they help flow into our lives has been called: Karma, Chi, Dua's, Blessings, and Angels.

Unseen forces can make two solid pieces of metals slam together or fly apart. These two pieces of magnets at their core are a bundle of energy made of atoms and neutrons and depending on what polarity they're focused on, the magnets can attract or repel each other.

Humans too are a solid package of energy made of atoms and neutrons at our **core**, like the magnets, we can attract a surge positive energy depending on what we focus on. We can use the power of our bodies, thoughts, and voice to capture and benefit from good forces. Billions of people for thousands of years have been using the written formulas assembled in this book to get good energy, given from generation to generation.

This is a collection of worldwide ways to attract Good Energy and repel bad energy. We all believe in a Higher Power, since we are all humans and **created equally**, we all come from the same Higher Power regardless of what we call our Creator.

Uniting worldwide energy **magnifiers** is like an energy drink containing a combination of caffeine, B vitamins and herbs. Like providing your home with wind, solar, and hydro electricity to help you super boost your power and be more efficient. Our Creator provided us with many elements on earth and prayers from Prophets thus joining them is like taking multi-vitamins.

Uniting all the good powers from earth to Heaven, to improve our life is what our Creator wants and what religions are based on, it's our **natural instinct**: Using blessings to protect and help ourselves and others uplift our physical, emotional, mental, and spiritual health.

Open Energy

What these spiritual scientists have in common with chemists, biologists and physicists is that they believe in the unseen and they devoted their lives to help others benefit from the flow of good energy from the unseen. If a scientist discovers a free open energy source that powers our home, we **don't discriminate** the color or country or religion where this scientist came from. In this same reverence, the formulas here to provide good energy for our lives are respected and appreciated without bias towards the scientists. All major religions teach we are all equal and some have been blessed with knowledge that can help humanity and it is our duty to share that knowledge.

Imagine holding up a long metal pole in a lightening storm, you will increase your chances of being struck by lightening, the energy you attract is indiscriminate, the energy does not avoid you based on your upbringing, the energy is attracted to you based on your actions. Similarly, fortune does not discriminate; it can come to anyone based on certain actions.

This book does not discriminate between the origin, religion, or ethnicity of the scientists, there is a common belief with the scientists that there is One Supreme Higher power, an **ultimate source** of the good energy, also called: Allah, God, Eli, etc., and that by practicing these Good Luck formulas, brings us closer to the higher power, such as Heaven, Nirvana, Paradise, Zion, Utopia.

In essence, worldwide Holy books are Good Luck books, helping the followers receive a good destiny and ultimately be closer to the Ultimate Highest Power. Therefore with an open mind, these Monks, Prophets, Wizards, are regarded as scientists helping us receive good energy and ultimately be with our Higher Power.

For example, the Quran states there is truth in the Gospel and the Torah, therefore, this book is not about the origin of the scientist or the name of the Supreme Power, it's about all of us benefiting as humans from the all the righteous ways to receive good energy and ultimately be with our Creator.

Various good luck methods are used by major religions, but because of prejudices, the good luck methods from different cultures have not been **bond together** to create a super good energy attraction force for you as done here.

More than half the world follows Abrahamic religions, using the same 10 Commandments **indiscriminately**. The largest religion being Islam, then Catholicism, then Protestants: All believing in Adam, Abraham, and Moses equally. The blessings and healing verses from the Holy books are called supplications, incantations, and dua's.

The Abrahamic religions have the **same intensions**, to attract good and repel evil. Certain verses are used by the Abrahamic religions for exorcisms, to expel bad forces from our lives and attract blessings from God. You can either combine or use the individual blessings that work best for you. All the religions promote researching and studying to expand your wisdom.

Some priests or elders shun the theory of "Good Luck", but they in fact promote and preach "good luck" calling it by different names. The act of saying certain words to elicit certain energy into your life is the act of practicing good luck in the name of our Creator. Nearly all religions are based on good luck, practicing certain codes to get certain fortunes.

This is not a proselytization to convert to another religion; you are free to choose the religion you want and to say the prayers or chants in the name of the higher power you believe in, for example, ask for the blessings in the name of Allah if Allah is the name you use for God. All religions believe that God sent Prophets around the world, that God helped guide all humans, so these prayers are from around the world, not exclusive to one culture or one group because God created all humans equal.

Prior to 2013, New York City officials adopted this tactic of combining good luck methods indiscriminately. Upon installing the 7-foot-tall number "13" for the "2013" ball drop on New Year's Eve in Times Square, the organizers made sure the number doesn't frighten off superstitious revelers by adding 13 "lucky" charms. "Some people get nervous about the number 13," said Tim Tompkins, president of the Times Square Alliance. "But just to keep all bases covered, we've gone ahead and gathered 13 good-luck charms — everything from a four-leaf clover to gold coins to bamboo to a Buddha statue," he said.

There is a saying that "there are **no atheists** in a battlefield fox hole", everyone believes in a higher power, regardless of the name of your Creator, all religions have many things in common, some are nearly identical with simply spelling variations for the name of God, one thing all belief systems have in common is asking the higher power for blessings through a set form of prayers, chants, or spells, categorized for you here.

First we have to have the **mindset** of getting good luck. If we don't focus on and acquire good energy, the consequence is by default getting bad energy, otherwise known as bad luck, gloom, depression, poverty, and despair. Instead of living a life that feels like Heaven, we can live a life that feels like hell. Thus it's urgent to center your thoughts and actions on getting good energy.

In addition to using spiritual and magical ways to attract good luck, there are practical ways to get good luck in your life now. First step is to create a system of being lucky. There has been scientific research comparing thousands of self proclaimed lucky and unlucky people with an **evident** difference between the two groups.

Make Good Luck

First you must work on your **practical good luck**! The research discovered that the people who described themselves as very lucky people live a vastly different lifestyle than people who call themselves very unlucky people.

1. Frequency of Trying

First, people who believe they have a lot of good luck actually make their own luck by applying themselves nearly twice as much as people who claim to be unlucky. For example, the lucky participants in the research did twice as much applying to jobs, entering contests, and marketing than the individuals who thought they were unlucky.

Therefore the lucky group got better jobs, won more contests, and succeeded more in business because they made nearly twice the effort to reach their goals. So the first way to increase your odds of being lucky is to take more chances. Buy more lotto tickets, apply to more jobs, and do more advertising, your chances of luck increases the more, the more good energy you put forward, the more good energy comes back to you, getting better luck in wealth.

2. Do not hide from luck

Second tactic the good luck people use to have a luckier life than the bad luck people is that they live a lifestyle of being extroverted. The bad luck people are statistically more introverted according to the research. The study showed that by being friendlier, you increase your good luck. Meeting more people opened up more opportunities including better luck in love.

The people who believe they have good luck smiled twice as much as unlucky people and engaged in far more eye contact. Furthermore, the lucky people used a more open body language, for example, not folding their arms or legs when talking to others and using open palm gestures.

3. Staying cool for luck

Third way lucky people were distinguished in the research is their level of calmness. Unlucky people behaved more tense and anxious. This affects your luck via your ability to perceive opportunities. When you are in a more relaxed pleasant state of mind, you can judge better if there is a good opening in front of you.

4. Experience luck

Fourth way lucky people live a different lifestyle than unlucky people is that lucky people try new experiences. They experiment with different foods and different sports and different methods of accomplishing things. For example, Thomas Edison is considered a very lucky man, but he failed 1,200 times prior to successfully creating the carbonized filament light bulb in 1879.

5. Exercise luck

Fifth way lucky people are different than unlucky people is the amount of time spent exercising. Many lucky people described using various forms of relaxation techniques to lower their stress levels whereas unlucky people don't spend as much time exercising. This raises your luck of being healthy. Exercising also increases our neurotransmitter receptor that triggers "electrical" signals in our body. By increasing our internal electricity, we can attract positive external electricity like a stronger magnet can pull more metal. Exercising also releases endorphins in our brain, a self made chemical that creates a feeling of well being and happiness. This is one of the major differences between the people who declare themselves lucky verses those who believe they are unlucky; the lucky people exercise more often.

6. Listen to luck

Sixth way the lucky people behaved different than the unlucky people is that they followed their instinct more often. The unlucky people went against their instincts of did not believe in their instincts so they made wrong decisions more often. We are blessed with internal radar like animals that sense fear or danger. Thus it's important to listen to our built in self defense mechanism more often.

The lucky people followed their intuition of someone being trustworthy or whether an opportunity was worthy, thus they were harmed less in life whereas unlucky people statistically went against their feelings more often. The lucky people trust themselves, whereas the unlucky people did not trust what their internal voice told them. The lucky people also take steps to listen to themselves more often by doing mental training such as meditation so they can listen to themselves more.

7. Expect good luck

Seventh difference between lucky people and unlucky people in the study is that lucky people expected good luck. This expectation is what gave them the fuel to keep trying over and over even when they failed, just like Thomas Edison. Unlucky people expected bad things to happen to them, thus either not even trying to succeed or even worse, self sabotaging themselves by sub-consciously making mistakes to self-fulfil their expectation to fail. This also extends to the unlucky people's interaction with people, for example, if they feel a person won't accept their social invitation, they won't even try to talk to the person. Whereas lucky people believe they will be liked so they talk to people more often.

This is a method of self affirmation that both groups do. Whereas the lucky group does the affirmations correctly and the unlucky people do affirmations that harm them. The key is to give yourself good luck affirmations, for example: Begin each day saying:

"I have good luck and I will have more good luck today".

"I am worthy of good luck and I will have more good luck today"

It may feel awkward to do this at first, but say it and believe it and see if it makes a difference for you. Also guard your mental integrity, only have good thoughts around you like a physical diet, have a mental diet, filter things and people who depress you and instead only have good thoughts and people and images around you.

8. Make Luck your Goal

Eighth way lucky people live a different lifestyle than unlucky people is the process of setting goals. Unlucky people less often wrote down and put of reminders of their life goals and plans whereas lucky people systematically lived by following their future written plans and goals. The lucky people decide on what their ideal life and dreams are and then put up reminders and steps to achieve those goals around them.

9. See Good Luck

Ninth way people with good luck lived different than people with bad luck is that when bad luck happened, the people with good luck perceived it as good luck. The good luck people saw everything as good luck because they acknowledge that regardless of what happens, there are other people who are less fortunate.

Therefore the good luck people do not over dramatize the bad luck and spiral into despair; instead they minimize it by still maintaining their self image of being lucky by comparing themselves to less lucky people. Furthermore, the good luck people look for the opportunity in the good luck as to how they can learn from it and use the experience to have better luck in the future. The unlucky people coil into depression and use the experience to affirm their bad luck, furthering their cycle of bad luck by expecting more bad luck.

Bouncing back and learning from experiences is key to increasing your good luck. Everyone makes mistakes and has accidents, or is hurt by others, but learning from them and being happy that it wasn't worse will help you maintain a good attitude that is the fuel for getting good luck. By dwelling on the misfortunes then the unlucky people are constantly draining their own energy and motivation from being fortunate. Even if someone has a bad day or week or month, the key is to think long term to have a good year, decade and life.

Good Luck in Love

Chinese Good Luck in Love

10. Good Feng shui to enhance your love life:

Place a lava lamp (fire), next to a bouquet of roses (wood) next to a clock (metal) next to a painting of fish (water) in the Southwest (the love sector) corner of your bedroom.

11. Feng shui to prevent love

Would be a fireplace (fire) placed next to a washing machine (metal) placed next to a palm tree (wood) placed next to a globe of the world (earth) placed next to a hot tub (water).

12. Feng shui To Protect love

As well as maintain good health you should make sure the bedroom adheres to the following general rules: The master bedroom should be as far away from the front Door as possible to provide a feeling of security and safety. The headboard of the bed should face either the family (west) or longevity (east) directions if possible. A person sitting in bed must be able to see who is entering the room (either by direct sight or using a mirror) this prevents the misfortune brought by negative chi from Sneaking up on you at night. The foot of the bed should NOT face the door because this is How the Chinese line up coffins for burial. It is considered to be the death position. It also should not face a mirror of a Bureau. The bed's headboard should not nudge the wall, but part of the bed should be touching a wall otherwise the people will feel unstable). Mirrored ceilings or mirrored closet doors are extremely bad Fortune in a bedroom, especially if they consist of mirrored Tiles.

13. **Feng shui to attract love**

    Make Space. There is an old saying that Love will not enter a home that is cluttered by piles of Newspapers, laundry or clotted with dust balls. The first Thing you should do is make sure that your southwestern Corners are not places where you store junk. Make sure that this area is spotless.

14. **Feng shui to attract love**

    Act As If You Already Have A Partner. One way to attract the Right soul mate into your sphere is to actually make room for them in your life. Make sure that your bed boasts a night Table on both sides of the bed. Make room in your closet for the clothes of your potential partner. If your bathroom is in the southwestern sector make sure it is spotless and filled with guest soaps and an extra toothbrush.

15. **Feng shui to attract love**

    Place Objects in Pairs. In your southwestern sector, solo Standing objects are a bad idea. Replace the freestanding Stuff with matching pairs of things: a set of love birds, a Couple of candles sticks or two hearts made of rose quartz. Paintings of two cranes, two mandarin ducks or two peony Blossoms are traditional Chinese decorations that are intended to bring a soul mate into your life. You can also hang classic romantic portraits of men and women courting Each other or other symbols of the birds and the bees in this Area. The Chinese symbol for "Double Happiness" or the Tai Chi symbol as well as the Western symbol of Venus and Mars Are also good images to hang in the love sector.

16. **Feng shui to attract love**

    Sensual items: If possible, fill this area of your home with sensual items such as chocolates candles, massage oils, Favorite perfumes and favorite foods. Think of the five senses here, and make sure you have catered to each as you try to augment this area.

17. **Feng shui to attract love**

    Tickle it Pink. In Feng shui, pink is the color of love. You can Paint this sector pink; soften it with flattering pink lighting, Pink candles, pink fabrics and a bowl of pink candies. The More pink the better! Even just a small touch of this love drawing color will help bring loving vibrations into your Personal sphere.

18. **Feng shui to attract love**

    Rounded and Curvy Items: Anything practical item that Boasts rounded curves such as an antique radio, art deco Perfume, nude bodies or an unusual piece of abstract art Works well in this sector. Lava lamps, particularly in pink or Rose colors, also assist in enhancing the energy of the love Sector. The exception is statues that feature a lone female Figure. No matter how sensuous it looks, opt for a statue that Features a couple embracing instead!

19. **Feng shui to prevent love**

    Stuff from Dead Relationships. Clean up the clutter of any Past romantic encounters from this area. Make sure you get rid of old love letters, gifts, trinkets and other mementos from what was once a happy relationship. This helps you

20. **Feng shui to prevent love**

    Depictions of Single Women: Remove all art in this area that depicts a single woman within the frame. This includes Portraits of you. Replace these images with pictures or Symbols of romantic couples.

21. **Feng shui to prevent love**

    Too much Yin or Yang: Try To balance your Southwestern corners out by adding a few masculine touches as well as the feminine ones. Conversely males should not boast southwestern corners filled with heaps of Sports equipment, dirty laundry or piles of girlie magazines. Clean the area up and try adding a feminine touch such as an Aromatherapy unit or a vase of flowers. If you leave this kind of clutter around it indicates to the cosmos that you are actually happy with your single lifestyle.

22. **Feng shui to prevent love**

    Childish Things: People stuck in codependent relationships that are looking for a parent often boast rooms filled with Stuffed animals, dolls and games. Eliminate this stuff and Replace it with less childish paraphernalia.

23. Feng shui to prevent love

Distractions: Remove items that make you stray from your Intent for a relationship, such as exercise equipment, your Office daybook, laundry and television. You can still keep these items, of course; just keep them out of the love area of your home.

24. Feng shui to prevent love

Sharp pointy things: Sharp angles and corners in this area of the home are thought to drive off potential suitors. This is not a great place to hang your collection of sabers, umbrellas or encourage the growth of a cactus.

Wiccan Good Luck in Love

25. Magic spell for More Joy and Love

Bring me love and bring me kisses,
Bring me joy and bring me fun,
Bring me perfect precious mornings
Every new day that's begun,
I am ready to receive now,
I am ready so let's go,
Bring me love and precious mornings,
Tis my will, now make it so.

26. Magic spell for Anti-loneliness

Here I am and I am me,
I am whole and I am free,
I am one and I'm a treat,
I am one and I'm complete.

Only one can laugh or cry,
Only one can bring and buy,
Only one can give me love,
Only one sun shines above.

I am here and I am free,
I decide my destiny,
Make my day and make my night,
Make them gorgeous, make them bright.

I am taking care of ME,
Help and comfort lovingly;
And no matter who YOU are -
I am ME, and I'm a STAR!

[And there, stand up, clap your hands, and call your own name, call yourself as your own and one true champion, and from that place of true acceptance and confidence, come up with something that will really please your loved one - you!]

27. Magic spell for letting go of a past love

You need: One large bowl of salt (cooking salt will do). A quiet place out of doors where you can walk for a while in a straight line without being disturbed. Do this ritual just before the sun sets/as the sun sets. Hold the bowl in one hand at the starting point of this "journey into the future". Say:

As this day sets with the sun,

Future's journey has begun.

I command thee:

Put my past behind me.

Take one step, a handful of salt and let a memory relating to the person come to you.

Throw the salt over your shoulder and say,

(Person's name, i.e.)
I send you
To the past
Where you
Belong,
Where you
Can do
No wrong.

Take a deep breath and another step. Take another handful of salt, and throw the next memory that comes up into the past, just the same. Continue until you can feel yourself getting lighter and clearer. When no more memories come up, the journey into the future is complete. Tip out the remaining salt from the bowl and say,

As the night will come,

All this is done.
Future's bright and clear for me,
As I will, so shall it be.

Walk AWAY from the trail of salt/trail of memories of the past (do NOT cross that path!) And let the wind blow it away as it will.

It is done.

Should at any time other thoughts or memories relating to the person appear that you didn't ask for or you don't want to think about, repeat THE SAME HAND GESTURE you made when you threw the salt with that hand, and the hand that held the bowl lies flat on the heart of magic (center of the chest).

If you can't go outdoors to do this for any reason, you can do this with IMAGINARY salt in a suitable room or hallway. It does work more profoundly with the real thing, however, and a real outdoors night; salt is magical stuff and very powerful.

28. Magic spell for Love Attraction

Featuring the Law of Three
Light a pink candle.

Focus on the person that is your example of love, and of which you want more in your life.

If your mind drifts, say to yourself out aloud and in your mind at the same time, "Only the love! Let me feel the love!" and focus on the sensations and feelings of loving someone/something with all your heart.

Remember that if you are using the law of three, the purer your vibration and the stronger your energy can be, the more powerful the good effects that come back to you in turn.

When you feel only love (admiration, wonderment, beauty, awesome, I love!) Take a deep breath and say:

I now call love into my life
According to the law of three
Love is my goal, love is my due,
Love is my will, so will it be.
Clap your hands three times, and then blow out the candle.

29. Magic spell for The Heart Healing

Place both your healing hands flat on the center of your chest, take a deep breath and speak the following words:

I place my own healing hands
On my own dear heart
With the gentleness
And with exquisite care;
The care I would afford
A tiny frozen bird
I found here on my doorstep.
Here, with my gentle healing hands
My touch brings warmth and life;
To right what once went wrong;
To heal what once was broken.
Fear not, my love.
I will do all I can do for you.
For sure, I am no angel
But what I have to give,
I give to you.

Jewish Good Luck in Love

30. Prayer to mend a broken heart

"He healeth the broken in heart, and bindeth up their wounds. He telleth the number of the stars; He calleth them all by their names" Psalm 147:3-4

31. Prayer for an easy end to a romance

Suggested incense: violet

"Now you have indeed gone away because you longed greatly for your father's house; but why did you steal my gods?" Genesis 31:30

32. Prayer to find forgiveness

Suggested incense: bayberry

"And ye shall eat in plenty and be satisfied, and shall praise the name of The Lord your God, that hath dealt wondrously with you; and my people shall never be put to shame." Joel 2:26

33. Prayer to find True and lasting love

Suggested incense: jasmine

"Many waters cannot quench love, neither can floods drown it: If a man would give all the substance of his house for love, He would utterly be scorned." Song of Songs 8:7

34. Prayer to open the eyes of those who will not see

Suggested incense: peppermint

"And it shall come to pass, if they will not believe even these two signs, neither hearken unto thy voice, that thou shalt take of the water of the river, and pour it upon the dry land: and the water which thou takest out of the river shall become blood up." Exodus 4:9

35. Prayer to protect a loved one

Suggested incense: coconut

"Yet even now, saith The Lord, turn ye unto me with all your heart, and with fasting, and with weeping, and with mourning: and rend your heart, and not your Garments, and turn unto The Lord your God; for he is gracious and merciful, slow to anger, and abundant in loving kindness, and repenteth him of the evil". Joel 2:12-13

36. Prayer to have your partner be a better lover

Prepare a red candle to attract.

"He brought me forth also into a large place; He delivered me, because he delighted in me" .Psalms 18:19

37. Prayer to be a better lover

Prepare a red candle to attract.

"And call upon me in the day of trouble; I will deliver thee, and thou shalt glorify me". Psalms 50:15

38. Prayer to stop someone from stealing your lover

Prepare a pink candle to repel.

"When I say unto the wicked, Thou shalt surely die; and thou givest him not Warning, nor speakest to warn the wicked from his wicked way, to save his life; the same wicked man shall die in his iniquity; but his blood will I require at thy hand." Ezekiel 3:18

39. Prayer to turn an enemy into a friend

Prepare a purple candle to attract.

"A time to cast away stones, and a time to gather stones together; a time to embrace, and a time to refrain from embracing." Ecclesiastes 3:5

40. Prayer to Make someone dream of you

Prepare a white candle to attract.

"My soul hath kept thy testimonies; and I love them exceedingly. " Psalms 119:167

41. Prayer for reconciliation

Prepare a blue candle to attract.

"And I will set the Egyptians against the Egyptians: and they shall fight every one against his brother, and every one against his neighbor; city against city, and kingdom against kingdom." Isaiah 19:2

42. Prayer to gain forgiveness

Prepare a blue candle to attract.

"And he said unto them, I am a Hebrew; and I fear the Lord, the God of heaven, which hath made the sea and the dry land". Jonah 1:9

43. Prayer to rid yourself of a bothersome lover

Prepare a pink candle to repel.

"May the glory of the Lord endure forever; May the Lord rejoice in His works, He looks on the earth, and it trembles; He touches the hills, and they smoke" I will sing to the Lord as long as I live; I will sing praise to my God while I have my being." Psalms 104:31-33

44. Prayer for new love and romance

"Fear not, for I am with you; be not dismayed, for I am your God; I will strengthen you, I will help you, I will uphold you with my righteous right hand." Isaiah 41:10

45. Prayer against Betrayal: -

"Yea, though I walk through the valley of the shadow of death, I will Fear no evil; For You are with me; Your rod and Your staff, they Comfort me." Psalms 23:4

46. Prayer for Marriage Blessings: -

"He who finds a wife finds a good thing, and obtains favor from the LORD." Proverbs 18:22

47. Prayer to reclaim lost destiny: -

"And Jabez called on the God of Israel saying, "Oh, that You would Bless me indeed, and enlarge my territory, that Your hand would be With me, and that You would keep me from evil, that I may not cause Pain!" So God granted him what he requested." 1 Chronicles 4:10

48. Prayer for the Unity of all Nations: -

"LORD, you will establish peace for us, for you have also done all our works in us." Isaiah 26:12

49. Prayer of Confidence: -

"For the LORD will be your confidence, and will keep your foot from being caught." Proverbs 3:26

50. Prayer for a Successful Marriage: -

"Therefore a man shall leave his father and mother and be joined to His wife, and they shall become one flesh´. Genesis 2:24

Christian Good Luck in Love

51. Prayer For new love and romance

Suggested incense: jasmine
"I may be able to speak the languages of human beings and even of angels, but if I have no love, my speech is no more than a noisy gong or a clanging bell. I may have the gift of inspired preaching; I may have all knowledge and understand all secrets; I may have the faith needed to move mountains-but if I have no love, I am nothing. I may give away everything I have, and even give up my body to be burned but if I have no love, this does me no good. L Corinthians, 13:1-13

52. Prayer against loneliness

Suggested incense: valerian
"Be sober, be watchful: your adversary the devil, as a roaring lion, walketh about, seeking whom he may devour, whom withstand steadfast in your faith, knowing that the same sufferings are accomplished in your brethren who are in the world. " 1st Peter 5:8-9

53. Prayer to impart kindness in a cold heart

Suggested incense: cedar
"And he answered and said unto them, He that hath two coats, let him impart to him that hath none; and he that hath food, let him do likewise." Luke 3:11

54. Prayer to find a better lover

Prepare a red candle to attract.

"For this is he, of whom it is written, Behold, I send my messenger before thy face, which shall prepare thy way before thee." Matthew 11:10

55. Prayer to rekindle the fire in a romance

Prepare a red candle to attract.

For to do whatsoever thy hand and thy counsel determined before to be done. -Acts 4:28

56. Prayer to stop a lover from cheating

Prepare a pink candle to attract.

"Through whom also we have had our access by faith into this grace wherein we stand; and we rejoice in hope of the glory of God. " Romans 5:2

57. Prayer to End an argument

Prepare a purple candle to repel.

"And set up false witnesses, which said, this man ceaseth not to speak blasphemous words against this holy place, and the law." Acts 6:13

58. Prayer to bring back a lost lover

Prepare a pink candle to attract.

"Ask, and it will be given to you; seek, and you will find; knock, and it will be opened to you. For everyone who asks receives, and the one who seeks finds, and to the one who knocks it will be opened." Matthew 7:7-8

59. Prayer to gain trust and favor

Prepare a white candle to attract.

"For the word of God is living and powerful, and sharper than any two edged sword, piercing even to the division of soul and spirit, and of joints and marrow, and is a discerner of the thoughts and intents of The heart; And there is no creature hidden from His sight, but all things are naked and open to the eyes of Him to whom we must give account." Hebrews 4:12-13

60. Prayer for Protection of Widows: -

"Now she who is really a widow, and left alone, trusts in God and Continues in supplications and prayers night and day." 1 Timothy 5:5

61. Prayer for Faithfulness: -

"And the apostles said unto the Lord, Increase our faith." Luke 17:5

62. Prayer for the Entire World: -

"And suddenly there was with the angel a multitude of the heavenly Host praising God and saying:"Glory to God in the highest, And on earth peace, goodwill toward Men!" Luke 2:13 – 14

63. Prayer of Confidence:

"And the apostles said to the Lord, "Increase our faith." Luke 17:5

Muslim Good Luck in Love

64. Prayer For love (Wife & Husband)

"Verily I have loved the good things besides the remembrance of my L ord. Until got hidden in the veil (of the darkness of the Night)".Quran 38: 32

65. Prayer for love (Wife & Husband)

"Them He loveth and they love Him. Lowly before the believers, mighty against the infidels." Quran 5:54

66. Prayer For love (Wife & Husband)

"Verily those who believe and work good deeds the Beneficent (God) will appoint love for them." Quran 19:96

67. Prayer for Light in your Heart

1. All the praises and thanks be to Allah, Who has sent down to His slave (Muhammad) the Book (the Qur'an), and has not placed therein any crookedness.

2. (He has made it) Straight to give warning (to the disbelievers) of a severe punishment from Him, and to give glad tidings to the believers (in the Oneness of Allah Islamic Monotheism), who work righteous deeds, that they shall have a fair reward (i.e. Paradise).

3. They shall abide therein forever.

4. And to warn those (Jews, Christians, and pagans) who say, "Allah has begotten a son (or offspring or children)."

5. No knowledge have they of such a thing, nor had their fathers. Mighty is the word that comes out of their mouths

[i.e. He begot (took) sons and daughters]. They utter nothing but a lie.

6. Perhaps, you, would kill yourself (O Muhammad) in grief, over their footsteps (for their turning away from you), because they believe not in this narration (the Qur'an).

7. Verily! We have made that which is on earth as an adornment for it, in order that We may test them (mankind) as to which of them are best in deeds. [i.e.those who do good deeds in the most perfect manner, that means to do them (deeds) totally for Allah's sake and in accordance to the legal ways of the Prophet].

8. And verily! We shall make all that is on it (the earth) a bare dry soil (without any vegetation or trees, etc.).

9. Do you think that the people of the Cave and the Inscription (the news or the names of the people of the Cave) were a wonder among Our Signs?

10. (Remember) when the young men fled for refuge (from their disbelieving folk) to the Cave, they said: "Our Lord! Bestow on us mercy from yourself, and facilitate for us our affair in the right way!" Quran 18:1-10

68. Prayer for Steadfastness of the heart

"Continue on the path you have been enjoined to follow, together with those who repented with you, and do not transgress." [Quran 11:112]

69. Prayer for a Spouse

"And (moreover) He has put affection between their hearts: not if you had spent all that is in the earth, could you have produced that affection, but Allah has done it: for He is Exalted in might, Wise" (Quran: 8:63)

70. Prayer for love

"On those who believe and work deeds of righteousness, will (Allah) Most Gracious bestow love". (Quran: 19:96)

71. Prayer to find a spouse

"Glory to Allah, Who created in pairs all things that the earth produces, as well as their own (human) kind and (other) things of which they have no knowledge". (Quran: 36:36)

72. Prayer for a spouse

Say: "If you do love Allah, Follow me: Allah will love you and forgive you your sins: For Allah is Oft-Forgiving, Most Merciful." (Quran: 3:31)

73. Prayer for Parents

"O my Lord! Forgive me, my parents, all who enter my home as a believer, and (all) believing men and believing women: and to the wrong-doers grant you no increase but destruction!" (Quran: 71:28)

74. Prayer for Parents

"O My Lord! grant me that I should be grateful for Your favor which You have bestowed on me and my parents, and that I should do good such as You are pleased and do good to me in respect of my offspring; surely I turn to You, and truly I submit (to You) in Islam." (Quran: 46:15)

75. Prayer for Parents

"My Lord! Bestow on them Your Mercy as they did bring me up when I was young." (Quran: 17:24)

76. Prayer For parents

"O our Lord! Forgive me and my parents, and (all) Believers, on the Day that the Reckoning will be established!" (Quran: 14:41)

77. Prayer For the return of someone who has absconded

78. Prayer for children

"And (O Allah), be gracious towards me in The matter of my off-spring. And surely, I have returned to you in repentance, and surely, I am of those who surrender (to you). Quran 46:15

79. Prayer for Piety in the family

"Our Lord, let our wives and offspring be a means of the coolness of our eyes and make us the leaders of the righteous people. Quran 25:74

80. Prayer for removing suspicion and doubt

"My Lord! I seek your protection from the prompting Of the Devils; and my Lord! I seek your protection from them approaching me. "Quran 23:97, 98

81. Prayer to get married

1. O Prophet! Fear Allah, and hearken not to the Unbelievers and the Hypocrites: verily Allah is full of Knowledge and Wisdom.

2. But follow that which comes to thee by inspiration from thy Lord: for Allah is well acquainted with (all) that ye do.

3. And put thy trust in Allah, and enough is Allah as a disposer of affairs.

4. Allah has not made for any man two hearts in his (one) body: nor has He made your wives whom ye divorce by Zihar your mothers: nor has He made your adopted sons your sons. Such is (only) your (manner of) speech by your mouths. But Allah tells (you) the Truth, and He shows the (right) Way.

5. Call them by (the names of) their fathers: that is juster in the sight of Allah. But if ye know not their father's (names, call them) your Brothers in faith, or your maulas. But there is no blame on you if ye make a mistake therein: (what counts is) the intention of your hearts: and Allah is Oft-Returning, Most Merciful.

6. The Prophet is closer to the Believers than their own selves, and his wives are their mothers. Blood-relations among each other have closer personal ties, in the Decree

of Allah. Than (the Brotherhood of) Believers and Muhajirs: nevertheless do ye what is just to your closest friends: such is the writing in the Decree (of Allah..

7. And remember We took from the prophets their covenant: As (We did) from thee: from Noah, Abraham, Moses, and Jesus the son of Mary: We took from them a solemn covenant:

8. That ((Allah)) may question the (custodians) of Truth concerning the Truth they (were charged with): And He has prepared for the Unbelievers a grievous Penalty.

9. O ye who believe! Remember the Grace of Allah, (bestowed) on you, when there came down on you hosts (to overwhelm you): But We sent against them a hurricane and forces that ye saw not: but Allah sees (clearly) all that ye do.

10. Behold! They came on you from above you and from below you, and behold, the eyes became dim and the hearts gaped up to the throats, and ye imagined various (vain) thoughts about Allah.

11. In that situation were the Believers tried: they were shaken as by a tremendous shaking.

12. And behold! The Hypocrites and those in whose hearts is a disease (even) say: "(Allah) and His Messenger promised us nothing but delusion!"

13. Behold! A party among them said: "Ye men of Yathrib! Ye cannot stand (the attack)! Therefore go back!" And a band of them ask for leave of the Prophet, saying, "Truly our houses are bare and exposed," though they were not exposed they intended nothing but to run away.

14. And if an entry had been effected to them from the sides of the (city), and they had been incited to sedition, they would certainly have brought it to pass, with none but a brief delay!

15. And yet they had already covenanted with Allah not to turn their backs, and a covenant with Allah must (surely) be answered for.

16. Say: "Running away will not profit you if ye are running away from death or slaughter; and even if (ye do escape), no more than a brief (respite) will ye be allowed to enjoy!"

17. Say: "Who is it that can screen you from Allah if it be His wish to give you punishment or to give you Mercy?" Nor will they find for themselves, besides Allah, any protector or helper.

18. Verily Allah knows those among you who keep back (men) and those who say to their brethren, "Come along to us", but come not to the fight except for just a little while.

19. Covetous over you. Then when fear comes, thou wilt see them looking to thee, their eyes revolving, like (those of) one over whom hovers death: but when the fear is past, they will smite you with sharp tongues, covetous of goods. Such men have no faith, and so Allah has made their deeds of none effect: and that is easy for Allah.

20. They think that the Confederates have not withdrawn; and if the Confederates should come (again), they would wish they were in the deserts (wandering) among the Bedouins, and seeking news about you (from a safe distance); and if they were in your midst, they would fight but little.

21. Ye have indeed in the Messenger of Allah a beautiful pattern (of conduct) for any one whose hope is in Allah and the Final Day, and who engages much in the Praise of Allah.

22. When the Believers saw the Confederate forces, they said: "This is what Allah and his Messenger had promised us, and Allah and His Messenger told us what was true." And it only added to their faith and their zeal in obedience.

23. Among the Believers are men who have been true to their covenant with Allah. Of them some have completed

their vow (to the extreme), and some (still) wait: but they have never changed (their determination) in the least:

24. That Allah may reward the men of Truth for their Truth, and punish the Hypocrites if that be His Will, or turn to them in Mercy: for Allah is Oft-Forgiving, Most Merciful.

25. And Allah turned back the Unbelievers for (all) their fury: no advantage did they gain; and enough is Allah for the believers in their fight. And Allah is full of Strength, able to enforce His Will.

26. And those of the People of the Book who aided them - Allah did take them down from their strongholds and cast terror into their hearts. (So that) some ye slew, and some ye made prisoners.

27. And He made you heirs of their lands, their houses, and their goods, and of a land which ye had not frequented (before). And Allah has power over all things.

28. O Prophet! Say to thy Consorts: "If it be that ye desire the life of this World, and its glitter,- then come! I will provide for your enjoyment and set you free in a handsome manner.

29. But if ye seek Allah and His Messenger, and the Home of the Hereafter, verily Allah has prepared for the well-doers amongst you a great reward.

30. O Consorts of the Prophet! If any of you were guilty of evident unseemly conduct, the Punishment would be doubled to her, and that is easy for Allah.

31. But any of you that is devout in the service of Allah and His Messenger, and works righteousness,- to her shall We grant her reward twice: and We have prepared for her a generous Sustenance.

32. O Consorts of the Prophet! Ye are not like any of the (other) women: if ye do fear ((Allah)), be not too complacent of speech, lest one in whose heart is a disease should be moved with desire: but speak ye a speech (that is) just.

33. And stay quietly in your houses, and make not a dazzling display, like that of the former Times of Ignorance; and establish regular Prayer, and give regular Charity; and obey Allah and His Messenger. And Allah only wishes to remove all abomination from you, ye members of the Family, and to make you pure and spotless.

34. And recite what is rehearsed to you in your homes, of the Signs of Allah and His Wisdom: for Allah understands the finest mysteries and is well-acquainted (with them).

35. For Muslim men and women,- for believing men and women, for devout men and women, for true men and women, for men and women who are patient and constant, for men and women who humble themselves, for men and women who give in Charity, for men and women who fast (and deny themselves), for men and women who guard their chastity, and for men and women who engage much in Allah's praise,- for them has Allah prepared forgiveness and great reward.

36. It is not fitting for a Believer, man or woman, when a matter has been decided by Allah and His Messenger to have any option about their decision: if any one disobeys Allah and His Messenger, he is indeed on a clearly wrong Path.

37. Behold! Thou didst say to one who had received the grace of Allah and thy favour: "Retain thou (in wedlock) thy wife, and fear Allah." But thou didst hide in thy heart that which Allah was about to make manifest: thou didst fear the people, but it is more fitting that thou shouldst fear Allah. Then when Zaid had dissolved (his marriage) with her, with the necessary (formality), We joined her in marriage to thee: in order that (in future) there may be no difficulty to the Believers in (the matter of) marriage with the wives of their adopted sons, when the latter have dissolved with the necessary (formality) (their marriage) with them. And Allah's command must be fulfilled.

38. There can be no difficulty to the Prophet in what Allah has indicated to him as a duty. It was the practice

(approved) of Allah amongst those of old that have passed away. And the command of Allah is a decree determined.

39. (It is the practice of those) who preach the Messages of Allah, and fear Him, and fear none but Allah. And enough is Allah to call (men) to account.

40. Muhammad is not the father of any of your men, but (he is) the Messenger of Allah, and the Seal of the Prophets: and Allah has full knowledge of all things.

41. O ye who believe! Celebrate the praises of Allah, and do this often;

42. And glorify Him morning and evening.

43. He it is Who sends blessings on you, as do His angels, that He may bring you out from the depths of Darkness into Light: and He is Full of Mercy to the Believers.

44. Their salutation on the Day they meet Him will be "Peace!"; and He has prepared for them a generous Reward.

45. O Prophet! Truly We have sent thee as a Witness, a Bearer of Glad Tidings, and Warner,-

46. And as one who invites to Allah's (grace) by His leave, and as a lamp spreading light.

47. Then give the Glad Tidings to the Believers, that they shall have from Allah a very great Bounty.

48. And obey not (the behests) of the Unbelievers and the Hypocrites, and heed not their annoyances, but put thy Trust in Allah. For enough is Allah as a Disposer of affairs.

49. O ye who believe! When ye marry believing women, and then divorce them before ye have touched them, no period of 'Iddat have ye to count in respect of them: so give them a present. And set them free in a handsome manner.

50. O Prophet! We have made lawful to thee thy wives to whom thou hast paid their dowers; and those whom thy right hand possesses out of the prisoners of war whom Allah has assigned to thee; and daughters of thy paternal

uncles and aunts, and daughters of thy maternal uncles and aunts, who migrated (from Makka) with thee; and any believing woman who dedicates her soul to the Prophet if the Prophet wishes to wed her;- this only for thee, and not for the Believers (at large); We know what We have appointed for them as to their wives and the captives whom their right hands possess;- in order that there should be no difficulty for thee. And Allah is Oft- Forgiving, Most Merciful.

51. Thou mayest defer (the turn of) any of them that thou pleasest, and thou mayest receive any thou pleasest: and there is no blame on thee if thou invite one whose (turn) thou hadst set aside. This were nigher to the cooling of their eyes, the prevention of their grief, and their satisfaction - that of all of them - with that which thou hast to give them: and Allah knows (all) that is in your hearts: and Allah is All- Knowing, Most Forbearing.

52. It is not lawful for thee (to marry more) women after this, nor to change them for (other) wives, even though their beauty attract thee, except any thy right hand should possess (as handmaidens): and Allah doth watch over all things.

53. O ye who believe! Enter not the Prophet's houses,- until leave is given you,- for a meal, (and then) not (so early as) to wait for its preparation: but when ye are invited, enter; and when ye have taken your meal, disperse, without seeking familiar talk. Such (behavior) annoys the Prophet: he is ashamed to dismiss you, but Allah is not ashamed (to tell you) the truth. And when ye ask (his ladies) for anything ye want, ask them from before a screen: that makes for greater purity for your hearts and for theirs. Nor is it right for you that ye should annoy Allah's Messenger, or that ye should marry his widows after him at any time. Truly such a thing is in Allah's sight an enormity.

54. Whether ye reveal anything or conceal it, verily Allah has full knowledge of all things.

55. There is no blame (on these ladies if they appear) before their fathers or their sons, their brothers, or their

brother's sons, or their sisters' sons, or their women, or the (slaves) whom their right hands possess. And, (ladies), fear Allah. For Allah is Witness to all things.

56. Allah and His angels send blessings on the Prophet: O ye that believe! Send ye blessings on him, and salute him with all respect.

57. Those who annoy Allah and His Messenger - Allah has cursed them in this World and in the Hereafter, and has prepared for them a humiliating Punishment.

58. And those who annoy believing men and women undeservedly, bear (on themselves) a calumny and a glaring sin.

59. O Prophet! Tell thy wives and daughters, and the believing women, that they should cast their outer garments over their persons (when abroad): that is most convenient, that they should be known (as such) and not molested. And Allah is Oft- Forgiving, Most Merciful.

60. Truly, if the Hypocrites, and those in whose hearts is a disease, and those who stir up sedition in the City, desist not, We shall certainly stir thee up against them: Then will they not be able to stay in it as thy neighbors for any length of time:

61. They shall have a curse on them: whenever they are found, they shall be seized and slain (without mercy).

62. (Such was) the practice (approved) of Allah among those who lived aforetime: No change wilt thou find in the practice (approved) of Allah.

63. Men ask thee concerning the Hour: Say, "The knowledge thereof is with Allah (alone)": and what will make thee understand?- perchance the Hour is nigh!

64. Verily Allah has cursed the Unbelievers and prepared for them a Blazing Fire,-

65. To dwell therein for ever: no protector will they find, nor helper.

66. The Day that their faces will be turned upside down in the Fire, they will say: "Woe to us! Would that we had obeyed Allah and obeyed the Messenger."

67. And they would say: "Our Lord! We obeyed our chiefs and our great ones, and they misled us as to the (right) Path.

68. "Our Lord! Give them double Penalty and curse them with a very great Curse!"

69. O ye who believe! Be ye not like those who vexed and insulted Moses, but Allah cleared him of the (calumnies) they had uttered: and he was honorable in Allah's sight.

70. O ye who believe! Fear Allah, and (always) say a word directed to the Right:

71. That He may make your conduct whole and sound and forgive you your sins: He that obeys Allah and His Messenger, has already attained the highest achievement.

72. We did indeed offer the Trust to the Heavens and the Earth and the Mountains; but they refused to undertake it, being afraid thereof: but man undertook it;- He was indeed unjust and foolish;-

73. (With the result) that Allah has to punish the Hypocrites, men and women, and the Unbelievers, men and women, and Allah turns in Mercy to the Believers, men and women: for Allah is Oft-Forgiving, Most Merciful." Quran Chapter 33

82. Prayer for mercy on family.

"Our Lord, forgive us and our brethren who were our forerunners in the faith, and do not put any ill feeling in our hearts toward the faithful. Our Lord, You are indeed most kind and merciful". (Quran 59:10)

83. Prayer for mercy on family.

"My Lord! Forgive me and my parents, and whoever enters my house in faith, and the faithful men and women, and do not increase the wrongdoers in anything except ruin". (Quran 71:28)

84. Prayer by Children for Parents.

"My Lord! Inspire me to give thanks for Your blessing with which You have blessed me and my parents, and that I may do righteous deeds which may please You, and invest my descendants with righteousness. Indeed I have turned to you in remorse, and I am one of the Muslims (those who submit). (Quran 46:15)

Good Luck Charms in Love

85. A Key

As a symbol of luck, a single key is among the most important, not to mention one of the oldest, of charms.

A key given as a gift between lovers is considered a symbol of unlocking the door to the heart. It is believed that the giver will be lucky in love.

The Greeks and Romans believed it represented the "Key of Life"

The ancients attached special significance to keys made of silver,

Among the Japanese, three keys tied together are considered a powerful lucky charm. They enable the wearer to unlock the doors that lead to love, health, and wealth.

According to the Gypsies of Eastern Europe, a door key with a metal ring attached will ensure a good night's sleep, if it is hung upside down over the bed. It will also prevent nightmares.

86. A Heart

Charms in the shape of hearts are obviously intended to bring luck in love.

In Christianity, the heart is seen as a representation of love and wisdom. In Egypt, the heart is seen as the center of our psychic energy and were thought to have power over the influences of black magic. Islam sees the heart as the basis of thought.

87. Munachi Amulet

for spells of love, passion, and desire, wrap hairs around the munachi figure, which depicts a copulating couple.

88. Norse sigil,

love charm to attract your most desired

89. Loving Friends Incense

1/2 part acacia

1 part rosemary

1/4 part elder

1/2 part frankincense resin

1 part dogwood

90. Attract a Lover Incense t

1 part lovage

1/2 part orris root (ground)

1 part lemon verbena

1/4 part patchouli

Few drops of lemon verbena oil

91. Attract Love Incense

1/2 part cloves

1 part rose

1/4 part saw palmetto

1/2 part juniper

Few drops of musk oil

Few drops of rose oil

1/2 part red sandalwood

92. To Attract Love:

Apple, Balm of Gilead, basil, caraway, Catnip, coriander, cowslip, dill, gardenia, Ginger, ginseng, honeysuckle, jasmine, Lavender, linden, marigold, marjoram,

Meadowsweet, mistletoe, myrtle, rose, Rosemary, valerian, vervain, violet (mixed with Lavender), yarrow

93. Attracting men:

Jasmine, juniper (dried berries
Worn as a charm), lavender, lemon verbena, Lovage, orris root, patchouli Attracting women: Henbane, holly, juniper (dried berries worn as a charm), lemon Verbena, lovage, orris root, patchouli

94. Pink candle

- Affection
- Romance
- Caring
- Nurturing
- Care for the planet Earth

95. Love stones.

Pink crystals in the shape of stars or hearts are Ideal Rose quartz, pink tourmaline, carnelian and pink Sapphires are good stones draw the positive energies Associated with love to you.

96. Feldspar

(also felspar) strengthens bonds of affection and promotes marital happiness; it is associated with fertility; mitigates quarrels and poor situations; protects from sunstrokes, headaches and nosebleeds.

97. Morganite

Induces love, devotion and friendship; promises career advancement or improved financial viability; reconciles difference of opinion and dispels anger; offers safety to travellers in any dimension.

98. Sardonyx

inspires love, romance and vitality; Helps confidence and fitness; ensures a result in Contractual difficulties; wards off infectious Disease; improves vision; heals fragile Relationships.

99. Azurite

commands social success and Friendship as well as constancy in love; improves Vision, both physically and psychically; protects From deceit and disillusion; affords help to those Faced with generative difficulties.

100.   Emerald

favors love and lovers, promising Constancy and fidelity; inspires confidence and Emotional fulfillment; strongly protective, Especially against deceit or delusions; ensures Safety of travellers and expectant mothers.

Manifest Good Luck in Love

101.   Manifest the image

Create a clear picture in your mind of your perfect partner. These vibrations can attract your imaginary man or woman into your life. Make a relationship collage with pictures of things that are important to you. Be specific when you visualize the environment and your future together.

102. Manifest the details

Put it in writing. Make a list of your needs and wants in a satisfying relationship. . Place the list where you can see it often. The more time and energy you devote to it, the closer the reality becomes.

103. Manifest the words

Focus on the list and verbalize it. Repeat it aloud for even greater impact. There's nothing like the power of the spoken word!

104. Manifest love in yourself

When you do not treat yourself the way you want others to treat You, you can never change the way things are. Your actions are Your powerful thoughts, so if you do not treat yourself with love and respect, you are emitting a signal that is saying you are Not important enough, worthy enough, or deserving. That signal will continue to be broadcast, and you will experience more Situations of people not treating you well. The people are just The effect. Your thoughts are the cause. You must begin to treat Yourself with love and respect, and emit that signal and get on That frequency. Then the law of attraction will move the entire Universe, and your life will be full of people who love and respect you.

Make and hold eye contact with yourself. You may feel a little uncomfortable at first but Let this pass and hold your own gaze in the mirror. Smile from ear to ear and say: "I love you." Don't just say it. Mean it! And proceed to tell yourself what a wonderful person you really are. Think of all the Reasons you love yourself and tell yourself with meaning and conviction. You must understand, fully and without question, the world is a better place because you Are in it. Acknowledge this to yourself and you'll soon begin to deeply deserving of all The things you wish to manifest.

Good Luck in Health

Chinese Good Luck in Health

105. Feng shui To improve your health,

Concentrate on the center area of your house by making sure Objects are placed in a clockwise fashion. An example for a Mantelpiece or dining room table would be a candle (fire) Placed next to a bowl of fruit (wood) placed next to silver salt And pepper shakers (metal) placed next to a vase filled with a Water and a flower (water)

106. Feng shui that prevents health,

You Might have objects creating a destructive cycle in the center of Your home. An example would be refrigerator (metal) adjacent To a stove (fire) adjacent to a table (wood) adjacent to a herb Garden (earth) adjacent to a sink (water).

107. Feng shui to Enhance the Health Sector

A collection of potted plants. The health sector of your home Is ruled by the earth element so pots of earth can help Stabilize and ground your health. Crystals and rocks. These objects belong inside the earth and Therefore correspond to the earth element.

108. Feng shui color for health

Brown, mustard and all shades of yellow. Sometimes all it Takes is a shift in color for you to effect a positive shift of chi. Tablecloths, curtains and floor coverings can supply these Colors. You can also paint the walls a shade of light brown to Yellow. Perhaps the simplest addition would be a pot of Bright yellow mums or chrysanthemums.

109. Feng shui shapes for health

Flat and square shaped forms and furniture. Squatter and More laterally shaped items suit this area well. Coffee tables Or short planters made of stone are examples of this kind of Structure.

110. Feng shui pictures for health

Pictures of Mountains or the World. A small globe or Photographs of mountainous regions also help emphasize the Theme of earth in this sector.

111. Feng shui fruit for health

Bowls of Fruit. In China, bowls of fruit placed in stone or Ceramic bowls are thought to enhance the health. A fruit bowl Created with real or ceramic peaches is a good addition to this Area as in China the peach is associated with longevity and Good health.

112. Feng shui symbols for health
Religious Objects. The center of the house is the best place to Put religious artifacts or build a small altar. If the

symbol is Made of stone, than the effect is Enhanced even more!

113. Feng shui humor for health

A Humorous Touch. An amusing knick-knack or a favorite Funny picture lifts the energies in this sector to keep you Light-hearted and connected to auspicious energies.

114. Feng shui that prevents health

Large Wooden Objects. Do not place a large wooden table, a Piano or any other huge wooden objects in your health sector. According to the cycles of production and destruction the earth element is Consumed by things that are wood. This includes religious Wooden statues, mantelpieces and hanging overhead beams.

115. Feng shui that prevents health

Columns. Things that are shaped like tree trunks or columnar In shape create stagnant energy in this sector. This is not a Good area to situate pillars,

116. Feng shui that prevents health

The Color Green. With the exception of the green that is Boasted by a small collection of healthy plants, the color Green hinders the good chi that is mainly produced by the Colors brown and yellow in the health sector.

117. Feng Shui for Fertility

Here are some quick tips on how to use Feng Shui to increase Your chances of conception (which of course is considered to be The ultimate creative act! Place the headboard of your bed so that it is against the Western wall of your bedroom.

118. Feng Shui for Fertility

Pictures of infants in silver frames placed on western walls Will help augment fertility. These can be pictures of you or Your spouse or pictures of close relatives.

119. Feng Shui for Fertility

A silver baby rattle placed in the western walls helps scare Away bad chi as well as appeal to the metal element.

120. Feng Shui for Fertility

Remove all old nails and do not hammer nails into the

Western walls of your home. A Feng shui superstition is that

Iron nails prevent conception. Use some other method of

Picture hanging instead.

121. Feng Shui for Fertility

Mobiles or chimes made of fluid aluminum shapes (think Alexander Calder) can also assist the process of conception.

122. Feng Shui for Fertility

A round metal or silver music box that plays a child's tune
Also attracts the fertile aspects of chi when placed against the Western walls of your home

Wiccan Good Luck in Health

123. Spell for Improving Vision, Clarity, Eyesight

Eyes of day
And eyes of night
Give me back
My own true sight
Let me see
Creator's light
Give me back my one true sight
See in sparkling clarity
This is my will, so shall it be.

124. Spell for Improving Hearing, Improving Clairaudience

Ears of mine
Now you hear
All the sounds
Crystal clear
Be they far
Or be they near,
All creation
Crystal clear
Range and resonance will grow
This is my will, now make it so.

125. Spell for Even Flow

Perfect body, perfect mind
Perfect heart and soul combined
I reclaim my Even Flow
Make it now and make it so.

Seasons turning, ocean tide
Sun and moon and Heavens wide,
Breathing in and breathing out,
Flow within and flow without.

As Creative wants for me
I am flow and harmony
I reclaim the Even Flow
Tis my will, now make it so.

126. Spell For Soothing A Stress Headache

Gently soothing gentle thoughts
Calm and clear, from far to near
Like a river to the bay
Soothing water, soothing thoughts,
Flow all darkness now away.

127. A Spell To Make Anything Healing

With your help,
My health shall grow,
As I will,
It shall be so.

128. Spell Against A Person Who Wishes You Harm

All acts of negativity
Will now return threefold to thee.

All bad you try to send my way
Upon your own self will hold sway.

All actions, thoughts and words of hate
Become your own decided fate.

By all up high, the worlds and wise
By oceans wide and deep blue skies
By day and night, and powers three
This is my will, so mote it be!

129. Spell for Healing

By my heart and by my soul,
What was broken,
Now make whole.

By my body, mind and soul
What was broken
Now make whole.

130. Spell against stress

Storms within
And storms without
Storms above

And storms below,
In my center
Only stillness
Its my will,
And it is so.

Jewish Good Luck in Health

131. Prayer To banish all that would do harm to you or any loved

one Suggested incense: rose

And be it still my consolation, Yea, let me exult in pain that spareth not, That I have not denied the words of the Holy One. What is my strength, that I should wait? And what is mine end, that I should be patient? Job 6:10-11

132. Prayer For protection in time of war

Suggested incense: angelica

But now, this is what the Lord says — he who created you, O Jacob, he who formed you, O Israel: "Fear not, for I have redeemed you; I have summoned you by name; you are mine. When you pass through the waters, I will be with you; and when you pass through the rivers, they will not sweep over you. When you walk through the fire, you will not be burned; the flames will not set you ablaze. Isaiah 43:1-2

133. Prayer For fertility

Suggested incense: musk

And he brought him forth abroad, and said, Look now toward heaven, and number the stars, if thou be able to number them: and he said unto him, So shall thy seed be." Genesis 15:5

134. Prayer To have a trouble free night of sleep

Prepare a white candle to attract.

And when the dew that lay was gone up, behold, upon the face of the wilderness a small round thing, small as the hoar-frost on the ground. Exodus 16:14

135. Prayer Always awaken fresh and full of energy

Prepare a red candle to attract.

And so it was, when the cloud abode from even unto the morning, and that the cloud was taken up in the morning, then they journeyed: whether it was by day or by night that the cloud was taken up, they journeyed. - Numbers 9:21

136. Prayer Enhance your powers physically and mentally

Prepare a red candle to attract.

And I will encamp about mine house because of the army, because of him that passeth by, and because of him that returneth: and no oppressor shall pass through them any more: for now have I seen with mine eyes. Zechariah 9:8

137. Prayer To overcome a strong enemy

Prepare a purple candle to repel.

And now thou sayest, Go, tell thy lord, Behold, Elijah is here. 1 Kings 18:11

138. Prayer Protection while traveling

Prepare a purple candle to repel.

He drew a circular horizon on the face of the waters, At the boundary of light and darkness, The pillars of heaven tremble. Job 26:10-14

139. Prayer To attract good health

I said to the boastful, 'Do not deal boastfully,' And to the wicked, 'Do not lift up the horn, Do not lift up your horn on high; Do not speak with a stiff neck,'" For exaltation comes neither from the east Nor from the west nor from the south, But God is the Judge: He puts down one, And exalts another. Psalm 75:4-7

140. Prayer to heal disease associated with old age

Praise the LORD, O my soul, and forget not all his benefits- who forgives all your sins and heals all your diseases, who redeems your life from the pit and crowns you with love and compassion, who satisfies your desires with good things so that your youth is renewed like the eagles." Psalm 103:2-5

141. Prayer to heal depression and anxiety

Praise the LORD. How good it is to sing praises to our God, how pleasant and fitting to praise him!

The LORD builds up Jerusalem; he gathers the exiles of Israel. He heals the brokenhearted and binds up their wounds." Psalm 147:1-3

142. Prayer to stop bleeding

"And when I passed by thee, and saw thee polluted in thine own blood, I said unto thee when thou wast in thy blood, Live; yea, I said unto thee when thou vast in thy blood, Live." Ezekiel 16:6

143. Prayer against the spread of venereal diseases: -

" and said, "If you diligently heed the voice of the LORD your God And do what is right in His sight, give ear to His commandments and Keep all His statutes, I will put none of the diseases on you which I Have brought on the Egyptians. For I am the LORD who heals you." Exodus 15:26

144. Prayer Against Natural Disasters -

Violence shall no longer be heard in your land, Neither wasting nor Destruction within your borders; But you shall call your walls Salvation, And your gates Praise." Isaiah 60:18

145. Prayer Against Fire outbreak: -

"You shall not be afraid of the terror by night, Nor of the arrow that Flies by day, Nor of the pestilence that walks in darkness, Nor of the destruction That lays waste at noonday." Psalms 91:5-6

146. Prayer for Little Children: -

"No more shall an infant from there live but a few days,

Nor an old man who has not fulfilled his days; For the child shall die One hundred years old, But the sinner being one hundred years old Shall be accursed." Isaiah 65:20

147. Prayer for Little Children: -

"Arise, cry out in the night, At the beginning of The watches; Pour out your heart like water before the face of the

Lord. Lift your hands toward Him For the life of your young children, Who faint from hunger at the head of every street." Lamentations 2:19

148. Prayer for Safe Delivery of Pregnant Woman:

"Shall I bring to the birth, and not cause to bring forth? Saith the LORD: shall I cause to bring forth, and shut the womb? Saith thy God." Isaiah 66:9

149. Prayer Against Boat Mishap, Air crash and Road Accident: -

"When you pass through the waters, I will be with you; And through The rivers, they shall not overflow you. When you walk through the Fire, you shall not be burned, Nor shall the flame scorch you." Isaiah 43:2

150. Prayer to fight every form of Social ills/vices in our Society: -

"Violence shall no longer be heard in your land, Neither wasting nor destruction within your borders; But you shall

Call your walls Salvation, And your gates Praise." Isaiah 60:18, 32:18

151. Prayer to fight every form of Social ills/vices in our Society: -

"My people will dwell in a peaceful habitation, In Secure dwellings, and in quiet resting places," Isaiah 32:18

152. Prayer for Quick Recovery from Sickness/Infirmity: -

"And the inhabitant will not say, "I am sick"; The People who dwell in it will be forgiven their iniquity." Isaiah 33:24

153. Prayer Against Spiritual Loss: -

"He swallows down riches And vomits them up again; God casts Them out of his belly." Job 20:15

154. Prayer for Protection: -

"No weapon formed against you shall prosper, And every tongue Which rises against you in judgment You shall condemn. This is the Heritage of the servants of the LORD, And their righteousness is from Me," Says the LORD." Isaiah 54:17

155. Prayer to End Violence: -

"He makes wars cease to the end of the earth; He breaks The bow and cuts the spear in two; He burns the chariot in the fire." Psalms 46:9

156. Prayer to End Violence: -

"He shall judge between many peoples, And rebuke Strong nations afar off; They shall beat their swords into plowshares, And their spears into pruning hooks; Nation shall not lift up sword Against nation, Neither shall they learn war any more. But everyone shall sit under his vine and under his fig tree, And no One shall make them afraid; For the mouth of the LORD of hosts has Spoken." Micah 4:3-4

157. Prayer for Good Health: -

"And said, "If you diligently heed the voice of the LORD your God and Do what is right in His sight, give ear to His commandments and keep All His statutes, I will put none of the diseases on you which I have Brought on the Egyptians. For I am the LORD who heals you." Exodus 15:26

158. Prayer Against Bad Luck:

"And He will destroy on this mountain The surface of the Covering cast over all people, And the veil that is spread over all Nations" - Isaiah 25:7

159. Prayer for Long life: -

"With long life I will satisfy him, And show him My salvation." Psalms 91:16

160. Prayer Against Miscarriage: -

"No more shall an infant from there live but a few days, Nor an old Man who has not fulfilled his days; For the child shall die one Hundred years old, But the sinner being one hundred years old shall Be accursed". Isaiah 65:20

161. Prayer against Untimely Death: -

"No more shall an infant from there live but a few days, Nor an old Man who has not fulfilled his days; For the child shall die one hundred years old, But the sinner being one hundred years old shall Be accursed". Isaiah 65:20

162. Prayer for Success in Examinations: -

"And he shall be like a tree planted by the rivers of water, that Bringeth forth his fruit in his season; his leaf also shall not wither; And whatsoever he doeth shall prosper". Psalms 1:3

163. Prayer to have babies (boys/girls): -

"For surely there is a hereafter, And your hope will not be cut off´." Proverbs 23:18

164. Prayer for fruit of the womb: -

"Then God blessed them, and God said to them, Be Fruitful and multiply; fill the earth and subdue it; have dominion over The fish of the sea, over the birds of the air, and over every living Thing that moves on the earth´." Genesis 1:28

165. Prayer for fruit of the womb: -

"You shall be blessed above all peoples; there Shall not be a male or female barren among you or among your Livestock´." Deuteronomy 7:14

Christian Good Luck in Health

166. Prayer To heal any sickness

Suggested incense: carnation

Ask, and it shall be given you; seek, and ye shall find; knock, and it shall be opened unto you: for every one that asketh receiveth; and he that seeketh findeth; and to him that knocketh it shall be opened. Matthew 7:7-8

167. Prayer to send healing energies to someone

Suggested incense: clove

And my God shall supply every need of yours according to his riches in glory in Christ Jesus. Philippians 4:19

168. Prayer to Contact your guardian angel

Prepare a purple candle to attract.

They are of the world: therefore speak they of the world, and the world heareth Them. 1 John 4:5

169. Prayer To send away bad health

Prepare a white candle to repel.

Do not think that I came to destroy the Law or the Prophets; I did not come to destroy but to fulfill; For assuredly, I say to you, till heaven and earth pass away, one jot or one tittle will by no means pass from the law till all is fulfilled. Matthew 5:17-18

170. Prayer to Heal from injuries and chronic pain

He himself bore our sins in his body on the tree, that we might die to sins and live for righteousness; by his wounds, you have been healed." 1 Peter 2:24

171. Prayer to Heal from warts and other growths

If we confess our sins, he is faithful and just and will forgive us our sins and purify us from all unrighteousness" 1 John 1:9

172. Prayer to heal for any kind of sickness

Is any one of you sick? He should call the elders of the church to pray over him and anoint him with oil in the name of the Lord. And the prayer offered in faith will make the sick person well; the Lord will raise him up. If he has sinned, he will be forgiven. Therefore confess your sins to each other and pray for each other so that you may be healed. The prayer of a righteous man is powerful and effective." James 5:14-16

173. Prayer for healing high blood pressure

Now, Lord, consider their threats and enable your servants to speak your word with great boldness. Stretch out your hand to heal and perform miraculous signs and wonders through the name of your holy servant Jesus. After they prayed, the place where they were meeting was shaken. And they were all filled with the Holy Spirit and spoke the word of God boldly." Acts 4:29-31

174.   Prayer for healing from infections

Let us draw near to God with a sincere heart in full assurance of faith, having our hearts sprinkled to cleanse us from a guilty conscience and having our bodies washed with pure water. Hebrews 10:22

175.   Prayer for Healing cold, flu and lung problems

In that day you will no longer ask me anything. I tell you the truth, my Father will give you whatever you ask in my name. Until now you have not asked for anything in my name. Ask and you will receive, and your joy will be complete." John 16:23-24

176.   Prayer for healing alcoholism

And these signs will follow those who believe: In My name they will cast out demons, they will speak with new tongues, they will take up serpents; and if they drink anything deadly they will recover; they will lay hands on the sick, and they will recover." Mark 16:17-18

177.   Prayer for healing stomach and eating disorders

"Ask and it will be given to you; seek and you will find; knock and the door will be opened to you. For everyone who asks receives; the one who seeks finds; and to the one who knocks, the door will be opened.

"Which of you, if your son asks for bread, will give him a stone? Or if he asks for a fish, will give him a snake? If you, then, though you are evil, know how to give good gifts to your children, how much more will your Father in heaven give good gifts to those who ask him! Matthew 7:7-11

178. Prayer for Safe Delivery of Pregnant Woman: -

"Nevertheless she will be saved in childbearing if they Continue in faith, love, and holiness, with self-control" 1 Timothy 2:15

179. Prayer to be strengthened in fasting

"Now it came to pass, as He was praying in a certain Place, when He ceased, that one of His disciples said to Him, "Lord, Teach us to pray, as John also taught his disciples." Luke 11:11

180. Prayer to be strengthened in fasting

"pray without ceasing," 1 Thessalonians 5:17

181. Prayer for Quick Recovery from Sickness/Infirmity: -

"But if the Spirit of Him who raised Jesus from the Dead dwells in you, He who raised Christ from the dead will also give Life to your mortal bodies through His Spirit who dwells in you." Romans 8:11

182.   Prayer Against Bad Luck:

"Beloved, I pray that you may prosper in all things and be In health, just as your soul prospers." 3 John 1:2

183.   Prayer to break barrenness: -

"For if these things are yours and abound, you will be neither barren Nor unfruitful in the knowledge of our Lord Jesus Christ'." 2 Peter 1:8

184.   Prayer to heal sickness/diseases: -

"Is any sick among you? Let him call for the elders of the church; and Let them pray over him, anointing him with oil in the name of the Lord; And the prayer of faith shall save the sick, and the Lord shall Raise him up; and if he have committed sins, they shall be forgiven Him'. James 5:14-15

Muslim Good Luck in Health

185.   Prayer For increase of breast milk

God Knoweth what every female beareth and that which the wombs fall shorts (of completion) and that in which they increase; and of everything (there is) with Him a measure The Knower of the unseen and the seen, the Great, the Most High." Quran 13: 8-9

186. Prayer for any sickness

You shall fight them, for GOD will punish them at your hands, humiliate them, grant you victory over them, and cool the chests of the believers. Quran [9:14]

187. Prayer for any sickness

O people, enlightenment has come to you herein from your Lord, and healing for anything that troubles your hearts, and guidance, and mercy for the believers" Quran [10:57]

188. Prayer for any sickness

Then eat from all the fruits, following the design of your Lord, precisely. From their bellies comes a drink of different colors, wherein there is healing for the people. This should be (sufficient) proof for people who reflect." Quran [16:69]

189. Prayer for any sickness

We send down in the Quran healing and mercy for the believers. At the same time, it only increases the wickedness of the transgressors." Quran [17:82]

190. Prayer for any sickness

"The One who created me, and guided me. - "The One who feeds me and waters me. - "And when I get sick, He heals me." Quran [26:78-80]

191. Prayer for Fever

Those who are righteous, whenever the devil approaches them with an idea, they remember, whereupon they become seers." Quran [7:201]

192. Prayer for Fever

"We said, "O fire, be cool and safe for Abraham." Quran [21:69]

193. Prayer for security against all harms

GOD is our Lord and your Lord. We have our deeds and you have your deeds. There is no argument between us and you. GOD will gather us all together; to Him is the ultimate destiny." Quran [42:15]

194. Prayer for security against all harms

"Nothing happens to us, except what GOD has decreed for us. He is our Lord and Master. In GOD the believers shall trust." Quran [9:51]

195. Prayer for security against all harms

If GOD touches you with a hardship, none can relieve it except He. And when He blesses you, no force can prevent His grace. He bestows it upon whomever He chooses from among His servants. He is the Forgiver, Most Merciful." Quran [10:107]

196. Prayer for security against all harms

There is not a creature on earth whose provision is not guaranteed by GOD. And He knows its course and its final destiny. All are recorded in a profound record." Quran [11:6]

197. Prayer for security against all harms

"I have put my trust in GOD, my Lord and your Lord. There is not a creature that He does not control. My Lord is on the right path." Quran [11:56]

198. Prayer for security against all harms

Many a creature that does not carry its provision, GOD provides for it, as well as for you. He is the Hearer, the Omniscient." Quran [29:60]

199. Prayer for security against all harms

If you ask them, "Who created the heavens and the earth?" they will say, "GOD." Say, "Why then do you set up idols beside GOD? If GOD willed any adversity for me, can they relieve such an adversity? And if He willed a blessing for me, can they prevent such a blessing?" Say, "GOD is sufficient for me." In Him the trusters shall trust." Quran [39:38]

200. Prayer for security against all harms

When GOD showers the people with mercy, no force can stop it. And if He withholds it, no force, other than He, can send it. He is the Almighty, Most Wise." Quran [35:2]

201. Prayer for protecting children against infantile diseases

"I have put my trust in GOD, my Lord and your Lord. There is not a creature that He does not control. My Lord is on the right path." Quran [11:56]

202. Prayer for healthy upbringing of children

He is the One who perfected everything He created, and started the creation of the human from clay. - Then He continued his reproduction through a certain lowly liquid. - He shaped him and blew into him from His spirit. And He gave you the hearing, the eyesight, and the brains; rarely are you thankful." Quran [32:7-9]

203. Prayer for Seeking Health

"Who created me, and It is He who guides me; Who gives me food and drink, And when I am ill, It is He who cures me; Who will cause me to die, And then to live (again); And who, I hope, Will forgive me my faults On the Day of Judgment". (Quran: 26:78)

204. Prayer for Seeking health

"And preserve them from (all) ills; and any whom You do preserve from ills that Day, on them will You have bestowed Mercy indeed: and that will be truly (for them) the highest Achievement". (Quran: 40:9)

205. Prayer for Seeking protection

"O my Lord! If it had been Your will You could have destroyed, long before, both them and me: would You destroy us for the deeds of the foolish ones among us? This is no more than Your trial: By it You cause whom You will to stray, and You lead whom You will unto the right path. You are our Protector: so forgive us and give us Your mercy; for You are the best of those who forgive. (Quran: 7:155)

206. Prayer for Seeking protection

"For my Protector is Allah, Who revealed the Book (from time to time), and He will choose and befriend the righteous". (Quran: 7:196)

207. Prayer for Seeking Protection

"You Creator of the heavens and the earth! You are my Protector in this world and in the Hereafter. Take You my soul (at death) as one submitting to Your will (as a (Muslim), and unite me with the righteous." (Quran: 12:101)

208. Prayer for General Well Being

"On no soul does Allah place a burden greater than it can bear. It gets every good that it earns, and it suffers every ill that it earns. (Pray:) "Our Lord! Condemn us not if we forget or fall into error; our Lord! Lay not on us a burden

Like that which You did lay on those before us; Our Lord! Lay not on us a burden greater than we have strength to bear. Blot out our sins, and grant us forgiveness. Have mercy on us. You are our Protector; Help us against those who stand against faith". (Quran: 2:286)

209. Prayer for general well being

"The Messenger believes in what has been revealed to him from his Lord, as do the believers. Each one (of them) believes in Allah, His Angels, His Books, and His Messengers. "We make no distinction (they say) between one and another of His Messengers." And they say: "We hear, and we obey: (We seek) Your Forgiveness, our Lord, and to You is the return (of all)." (Quran: 2-285)

210. Prayer for general well being

Say: "O my Lord! Let my entry be by the Gate of Truth and Honour, and likewise my exit by the Gate of Truth and Honour; and grant me from Your Presence an authority to aid (me)." (Quran: 17:80)

211. Prayer for General well being

"Our Lord! Give us in this world that which is good and in the Hereafter that which is good, and save us from the torment of the Fire!" (Quran: 2:201)

212. Prayer for When fearing an attack from an animal

Allah is our Lord and your Lord. For us is our deeds and for you, yours. There is no argument between us and you. Allah will bring us together. " Quran 42:15

213. Prayer to prevent entering the house

Indeed, I rely in Allah, my Lord and your Lord. There is no animal but He grasps it by its forelock. Surely, my Lord is on the Straight Path. Quran 11:56

214. Prayer to protect against snakes

Surely your Lord is Allah, Who created the heavens and The earth in Six periods, then established Himself on the Throne (of high Authority) befitting His Supreme Majesty. He covers the night and the day by each other following swiftly; And (He created) the sun and the moon and the stars, All subservient to His Command. Listen! His is the Creation and His is the Command. Blessed is Allah, the Lord and Cherisher of all the Worlds! Call on your Lord in all humility and in secrecy and Surely Allah loves not these who trespass limits. And do not make mischief in the earth after it has been set Right and call on Him fearing and hoping (in your heart of hearts). Surely the Mercy of Allah is nigh to the doers of good." Quran 7:54,56

215. Prayer to protection against animals

And their dog stretching forth his Two fore-legs on the threshold." Quran 18:18

216. Prayer for Insomnia

Surely, Allah and His angels send salawaat (blessings) on the Nabi. O you who believe, (you too) send salawaat and salutations on him." Quran 33: 56

217. Prayer for Bone fracture

But if they turn away, say: 'Allah suffices me: There is none worthy of worship but He: upon Him is my trust — He is Lord of the Great Throne." Quran 9:129

218. Prayer for Itching of the body

And We clothed the bones with flesh; Then We made it into another creature. Thus exalted is Allah, The Best of Creators. Quran 23:14

219. Prayer for Inflammation of the eyes

Allah is the Light of the heavens and the earth. The likeness of His light is as a niche wherein is a lamp, That lamp is in (a chandelier of) glass, the chandelier is as a Star glittering like a pearl lit from a blessed olive tree, Neither eastern nor western, whose oil is almost luminous Even though no fire touches it. (This) is all light upon light! Allah guides unto His light whom He will. And Allah sets forth all manner of Parables for (the guidance of) mankind. And verily Allah is Best Knower of all things. In the houses (of worship) which Allah has ordered to be exalted, And His name to be remembered therein - extol His Glory Therein in the mornings and the evenings - By men whom neither trade nor business diverts from the Remembrance of Allah, and the establishing of prayer And the paying of the poor-rate (Zakaat). They keep fearing the Day when hearts will be Unnerved and eyes convulsed (with terror)- That Allah may recompense them for their best deeds, And may grant them still more out of His Grace. And Allah provides for those whom He will, without measure." Quran 24:35,39

220. Prayer for Strengthening the eyesight

"Now We have removed from you your veil and This day your sight is iron." Quran 50:22

221. Prayer for Headaches

"Where from they get no aching of the head nor any madness." Quran 56:19

222. Prayer For a specific pain

With truth have we revealed it and with truth It has descended. And we have not sent you But as a bearer of good tidings and as a warner." Quran 17:105

223. Prayer for Disease of the spleen

Lo! Allah grasps the heaven and the earth that they deviate not. And if they were to deviate there is not one That could grasp it after that. Lo! He is For-Ever Clement, Forgiving." Quran 35:41

224. Prayer for palpitation of the heart

Do they seek (a religion) other than the Religion of Allah? Yet to Him has submitted whosoever is in The heavens and in the earth, willingly or unwillingly, And to Him shall they (all) be brought back in the end. Say (O Muslims!): "We believe in Allah and what has been Sent down to us, and that which was sent down to Abraham and Ishamael and Isaaq and Jacob and their offspring and what was given To

Moses and Jesus and the other Prophets from their Lord. We make no distinction between any of them, in the matter Of faith and to Allah have we surrendered ourselves." And whosoever seeks a religion other than Islam, It shall certainly not be accepted of him; And in the Hereafter he shall be of the losers. " Quran 3: 83,85

225. Prayer for protection of a vessel

In the Name of Allah be its course and its mooring. Lo! My Lord is Most Forgiving, Ever Merciful. Quran 11: 41

226. Prayer for When the seas are rough

Have you not seen how the ships glide on the sea by Allah's grace that He may show you of His wonders! Lo! Indeed, therein are signs for every steadfast, grateful (soul)." Quran 31:31

227. Prayer for Improving the memory

My Lord! Expand for me my bosom. Ease my task for me. Remove the knot from my speech so that They may understand what I say." Quran 20: 25,28

228. Prayer for safety in travelling

And say, "My Lord! Admit me with a worthy entrance, and bring me out with a worthy exit, and give me a favorable authority from Yourself." Quran (17:80)

229. Prayer for mercy and removal of difficulties.

He said, "My Lord! I seek Your protection in case I should ask You something of which I have no knowledge. If You do not forgive me and have mercy upon me I shall be among the losers." Quran (11:47)

230. Prayer for mercy on family.

Our Lord! You comprehend all things in mercy and knowledge. So forgive those who repent and follow Your way and save them from the punishment of hell. Quran (40:7)

231. Prayer for mercy and removal of difficulties.

Our Lord! Indeed You know whatever we hide and whatever we disclose, and nothing is hidden from Allah on the earth or in the sky. Quran (14:38)

232. Prayer for protection during war

Our Lord! Do not make us a (means of) test for the wrongdoing group, Quran (10:58)

233. Prayer for protection during war

and deliver us by Your mercy from the faithless group. Quran (10:86)

234. Prayer for protection during war

Our Lord, forgive us our sins, and our excesses in our affairs, and make our feet steady, and help us against the faithless group." Quran (3:147)

235. Prayer for protection during war

Our Lord, pour patience upon us, make our feet steady, and assist us against the faithless group." Quran (2:250)

236. Prayer for regaining health

Our Lord! Perfect our light for us, and forgive us! Indeed You have power over all things. " Quran (66:8)

237. Prayer for safety.

Our Lord! Pour patience upon us, and grant us to die as Muslims. Quran (7:126)

Good Luck Charms in Health

238. A Wheel

The flag of modern India has Buddha's Wheel of Life as its centerpiece. It was said that Buddha himself drew such a wheel in a rice field to teach his followers that all creation is a series of causes and effects following each other like the turning of a wheel.

239. A circle

representing eternity, the wheel appears frequently as a lucky charm in many cultures. It symbolizes that bad luck passes and good luck rises, just as a wheel is turned.

240. A Triangle

In engineering, the triangle is considered the strongest and most indestructible form for structures of every description. Even before mankind began to realize this, practitioners of ancient religions found mystical significance in the shape of a triangle and frequently fashioned charms and amulets in that shape.

It was perceived as representing the cycle of life -birth, maturity and death- and as such it stood for the harmony of humans with their gods. It was considered a sacrilege to break its perfect shape.

The ancient Egyptians used this holy shape when they created the great pyramids, which many today regard all by themselves as symbols of good luck, even though they are in reality monuments of dead. The architects who designed them combined four triangles as a symbol of the coming together of the forces of earth and of heaven.

241. A Crescent

Among the most powerful of all lucky symbols, the crescent is especially lucky for young children and their mothers.

In ancient Egypt, the crescent moon was the symbol of Isis, the Mother of the Gods. As its symbolism spread throughout the world, it eventually became a symbol of paradise, when represented with a star. It is particularly significant in Islam.

242.   A Sapphire

The sapphire has been a symbol of good luck since the most ancient of times.

The Greeks believed that to wear the sapphire was to invite the favor of the gods.

In the ancient Middle East, this blue stone was believed to have supernatural powers. It was said to have been the centerpiece of King Solomon's ring.

In India, it has the power to bring health and wealth.

243.   Lucky bamboo

is used to attract health, happiness, love and abundance.

A Rabbit's Foot The hind foot of a rabbit been a good luck symbol for the common man for ages.

Because of the rabbit's reputation in procreation, it is said to enhance the chances of the wearer to become a parent. When the rabbit's foot is worn by a man, he shall sire a child. When worn by a woman, she will become pregnant.

244. Turtles

Turtles are believed to have Power over all kinds of Bad Magic. A Turtle symbolizes the primal mother and Mother Earth. Turtles are also said to symbolize Longevity and one's Hope and Wish for a long life.

245. Tortoises

Tortoises are considered a good luck symbol in Feng-Shui decorating. They are also one of the 4 sacred animals (among the Dragon, Unicorn, and Phoenix) it is famous for longevity and strength, common traits found in many cultures.

246. Dolphins

Dolphins are considered lucky in many different cultures, including the Ancient cultures of Greece, Sumer, Egypt, and Rome.

For Christians and Native Americans, the Dolphin is a symbol of protection, and its image is said to bring good luck. The belief stems from the fact that ancient sailors who spent months or even years out of sight of land, found the sight of Dolphins swimming around their ships to be the first sign that land was near.

247. Eggs

In traditional folk religion, the Egg is a powerful symbol of fertility, purity and rebirth.

It is used in magical rituals to promote fertility and restore virility; to look into the future, to bring good weather, encourage the growth of crops and protect both cattle and children against misfortune, and ward off the evil eye.

248. A Cricket

on the hearth has been a sign of household luck for thousands of years.

This belief could stem from prehistoric times, when a Cricket's chirping provided a kind of companionship.

In China and other Asian countries, the cricket served as a watchdog: at any sign of danger, the chirping will stop. In the Far East as well as across Europe, it is considered very bad luck to kill a cricket, even by accident.

Almost every Native American tribe believed the Cricket, a bringer of luck, and they thought that imitating it's chirp was disrespectful.

Images of Crickets appear on charms and amulets, particularly those intended to ward off the evil eye, in ancient cultures of the Middle East and Europe.

249. Healing Incense

2 parts myrrh resin

1 part cinnamon

1 pinch saffron

250. Healing Incense

1 part rose

1 part eucalyptus

1 part pine

1 pinch saffron

251. Healing Incense
1 part rosemary
1 part juniper
When used in oil form – that is, on a tissue placed on
A radiator or in a burner – this incense is easily used
In a hospital environment.

252. Regain Health Incense
3 parts myrrh resin
2 parts nutmeg
1 part cedar
1 part clove
1/2 part balm
1/2 part poppy seeds
Few drops of pine oil
Few drops of sweet almond oil

253. For Healing:
Aloe, ash, camomile, cinnamon,
Comfrey, eucalyptus, fennel, garlic, hops,
Marjoram, mint, nettle, pine, rosemary, saffron,
Sage, sandalwood, thyme, yarrow

254. For Fertility:
Acorns, geranium, hawthorn,

Mandrake, orange (dried and powdered peel),
Pine, poppy, sage, sunflower (seeds)

255. Green candle
- The Element of Earth
- Physical healing
- Monetary success
- Mother Earth
- Tree and plant Magic
- Growth
- Personal goals

256. Agate
Promotes good health and fortune; increases physical stamina and brings benefits through wills or legacies; repels anger, mistrust and enmity; affords protection against rumor and gossip.

257. Aventurine
promotes health, vigor and Cheerfulness; it promises emotional moral Support in new commercial undertakings; gets Rid of doubt, diminishes anxiety and eases Bodily aches and pains; strengthens resolve Against hardship.

258. Jade
promotes good health and good situations; Favors artistic and musical endeavors; dulls Pain and helps soundness of sleep; also improves a poor memory; and is strongly Protective.

259.   Sapphire

affords good health, strength and Efficiency; heightens perception and rewards Commercial and social efforts; is strongly Protective against antagonism and malice; Effects reconciliation between lovers.

260.   Tiger's eye

defeats the opponent and ensures Victory in any competitive situation; Commands love and loyalty; offers protection from treachery and deception; strengthens the Body's immune system.

Manifest Good Luck in Health

261.   Manifest laughter

Illness is just the weak link. As a result of One thing: stress. If you put enough stress on the chain and You put enough stress on the system, then one of the links Breaks.

All stress begins with one negative thought. One thought that went Unchecked, and then more thoughts came and more, until stress is manifested. into illness.

The key to counter the stress is Laughter and joy to dissolve disease in our bodies. There are many testimonies of people with illnesses as bad as cancer who have self cured themselves by focusing purely on laughter.

By watching and listening to comedy continuously, and feeling happy and joyous all day, they were cured. If you have a disease, and you're focusing on it, and you're talking to people about it, you're going to create more diseased

262.   Manifest a perfect body

See yourself living in a perfectly healthy body. Hospitals sometimes give placebo (fake) pills that patients believe is the real pill and the patients are cured because they believed it is a real pill. When patients believe they are being cured, their bodies actually heals itself like a wound healing itself.

"Focusing on perfect health " is something we can all do within ourselves, despite what may be happening on the outside. So instead of talking about illness, change the conversation to good things, and give powerful thoughts to seeing those people in health.

Good Luck in Wealth

Chinese Good Luck in Wealth

263.   Feng shui to attract fame

To become famous you would enhance the Southern wall of your home by painting it red and then placing Red lights (fire) next to a bunch of bamboo (wood) next to a Trophy (metal) next to fountain (water).

264.   Feng shui that prevents wealth

Destructive cycle that could cause poverty is the Placement in the Southwest or North of a candle (fire) next to a Computer (metal) next to a painting of flowers (wood) next to an Ashtray (ashes are earth) next to a washroom (water.)

265.   Feng shui to attract wealth

The kitchen is very important as it is a symbol of your

Family's wealth and prosperity. The placement of the stove is most important in Feng Shui. It Should be positioned so a person using it can see who is Entering the room (either by direct sight or using a mirror). The cook must not be surprised by someone coming into the Room because it may cause accidents or affect food . The stove should NOT face: the front door, bathroom door, Master bedroom door or a staircase It should not be placed Directly beneath a bed on another floor under a beam, or in a Corner.

The stove should not be directly placed next to a water or

Metal element such as the kitchen basin. There should be ample room to work around the stove - it Should be kept clean and work well to encourage favorable Finances.

266. Feng shui to attract wealth

In Feng Shui water is symbolic of money so the first thing

You should do before you buy any house or apartment is check the water pressure! If you turn on a tap and the water

Flows out in a trickle then you are likely to experience financial Problems during your stay there.

267. Feng shui to attract wealth

There is just no good place to have a toilet Positioned in your house. Wherever the toilet is positioned you Are most likely to experience losses in your life. For instance, if The toilet positioned in your Southwest Corner which represents Love and relationships it can cause negative energy in that area Of your life. The same goes for any other area in the home that

The toilet is located. A Feng shui remedy for this problem is to keep the lid of the Toilet closed at all times to prevent your fortunes from being Flushed away! Another radical remedy is to place a small set of Metal chimes on the handle of the toilet to negate the bad Energy each time you flush.

268. Feng shui that prevents wealth

The bathroom should NOT be located in the wealth, fame, or Career sectors of the home, nor should it be visible from the Front door. The bathroom should be clean, well lit, well ventilated, and Have many mirrors. Make sure the mirrors don't reflect the Toilet but rather the places from which water flows INTO the Home such as the shower and the sink. The toilet should be hidden, if possible in a separate room, And not be placed in a central part of the home because it Could "flush away" opportunity.

269. Feng shui that prevents a Good Reputation

The Southeastern sector of your home is not a good place to put a Fountain or an aquarium. Water weakens and destroys fire Energy.

270. Feng shui that prevents a Good Reputation

Black, navy blue and other dark colors Compromise the fiery energy of the fame area. You want to Keep this area decorated in rosy tones and brightly lit.

271. Feng shui that attracts Opportunity

If your desire is to explore the world place Images of planes trains and far away exotic places in the Southeastern sector of your home.

272. Feng shui that attracts Opportunity

The Southeastern sector of your home is an ideal place to store your Educational books especially Atlases and self-help books.

273. Feng shui that attracts Opportunity

Maps of the World. Setting a rotating globe or a map of the World in the Southeastern sector of your home can help increase your chances of travel.

274. Feng shui that attracts Opportunity

Bells. The Southeastern sector of your home in which you can hang bells on a
Ribbon or display a collection of bells

275. Feng shui that attracts wealth

Career (The North Wall of your home) If you can't find a job, hate your job or feel like you are Constantly looking at a glass ceiling then look to the Northern Sector of your home to examine the chi and figure out why you Are "swimming against the current." Things that Enhance Your Career: Water. The North is ruled by flowing water so this is the Perfect place to install a tabletop fountain.

276. Feng shui that attracts wealth

Black objects work well in (The North Wall of your home) as Black is the color that symbolizes water in Chinese Feng Shui.

277. Feng shui that attracts wealth

Mirrors also equal water in Feng shui, so the Placement of mirrors in (The North Wall of your home) not only doubles your Chance of success but also increases the chi that is Appropriate to flow through this area.

278. Feng shui that attracts wealth

Place images that Represent the lifestyle or occupation that you aspire to in (The North Wall of your home). A writer for instance should place a picture of his or Favorite author or your favorite inventor.

279. Feng shui that attracts wealth

The fluidity of glass is comparable to the fluid Movement of water. Feel free to enhance your career energies By placing glass vases, shelves and bowls in (The North Wall of your home).

280. Feng shui that prevents wealth

Earth in (The North Wall of your home). Is This is not the area to keep potted plants. Dirt has the Effect of muddying the water element in this area. Also avoid Using anything made of clay or ceramic in this area as these Materials represent the Earth element.

281.   Feng shui that prevents wealth

Yellow and earth-toned colors are too earthy for this

Water (The North Wall of your home).. Keep the tones as white and black as Possible with a lot of glass elements.

282.   Feng shui that prevents wealth

Avoid Square Shapes. In (The North Wall of your home).. Squares represent earth in Feng shui And are hostile to the earth element. Look for furniture that Has a curvaceous design and boasts rounded corners. Counterbalance tables, shelves and flat counters by placing Objects with undulating forms on them, such as glass Sculptures and glass bowls.

Wiccan Good Luck in Wealth

283.   Money Energy Spell

Money gold and silver bright
Stream towards me in the night
Stream towards me in the day
Like a river to the bay
Easy, fun and joyous light
Money gold and silver bright
I await you, come to me
As I will, so shall it be!

284. Spell for Understanding Money

A powerful force
In the world of man
I open myself
To learn all that I can
I now lay aside
All I thought that I knew
And I learn all there is
Bright and true, fresh and new
I don't judge any longer
Free myself of the old
And I call on the force
And the power of gold
Tell and teach me and reach me
So that I might
Use this power for all
That is good, that is right

By the future and past
By the sun and the rain
By the stars and the sunrise
That will come yet again,
Let my knowledge and wisdom
Of money now grow
This is my will, so now make it so.

285. Spell for attracting money

Money joy and money pleasure,

Money riches, money treasure,

Come to me my friend of old

Come to me in shining gold,

I'm in love for I can see

You are perfect energy!

Feed me, lift me, bring me joys,
Bring me pleasures, bring me toys,
Rushing brightness I adore,
Clear me, raise me, more and more!
Money come and play with me!
I invite you - 1 - 2 - 3 !

Now, REALLY clap and cheer:
Yeah!
Money!!!
We LOVE money!!!
Whoohooo!

You will need:
One green candle.
Three silver coins.
Salt.

286.   Spell for attracting wealth

Money in my pocket
And money in my hand
Money in my home
And money in my bank

Money streams towards me
Like the river to the sea

Its easy and its wonderful
As counting 1-2-3!

...and ...

There's money in my pocket
And money in my hand,
Money in my home
And money in my bank.

Wherever I shall go
And whatever I may do
I clearly state the fact
Its true and it is so!

Money streams towards me
Like the river to the sea
Its easy and its wonderful
As counting 1-2-3! .

Jewish Good Luck in Wealth

287.   Prayer To find lost money

Suggested incense: marigold

Go, and cry in the ears of Jerusalem, saying, Thus saith The Lord, I remember for thee the kindness of thy youth, the love of thine espousals; how thou wentest After me in the wilderness, in a land that was not sown. Jeremiah 2:2

288.   Prayer That debts will be repayed

Suggested incense: almond

Do not rob the poor because he is poor, nor oppress the afflicted at the gate; for the Lord will plead their cause, and plunder the soul of those who plunder them.

Proverbs 22:22-23

289. Prayer For luck with the lottery

Suggested incense: chamomile

Honor the Lord with your possessions and with the first fruits of all your increase; so your barns will be filled with plenty, and your vats will overflow with new wine. Proverbs 3:9-10

290. Prayer To attract wealth

Suggested incense: ginger

Ask me, and I will give you the nations as your inheritance and the ends of the Earth as your own possession. - Psalms 2:8

291. Prayer For success in making money

Suggested incense: cinnamon

Bring ye all the tithes into the storehouse, that there may be meat in mine house, and prove me now herewith, saith the Lord of hosts, if I will not open you the windows of heaven, and pour you out a blessing, that there shall not be room enough to receive it. Malachi 3:10

292. Prayer To protect your home from fire

Suggested incense: hazel

The Lord watches over you—the Lord is your shade at your right hand; the sun will not harm you by day, nor the moon by night. The Lord will keep you from all harm—he will watch over your life; the Lord will watch over your coming and going both now and forevermore. Psalm 121:5-8

293. Prayer for Favors from important people

Suggested incense: patchouli

I communed with mine own heart, saying, "Lo, I have come to great estate, and have gotten more wisdom than all they that have been before me in Jerusalem; yea, my heart had great experience in wisdom and knowledge." Ecclesiastes 1:16

294. Prayer To stop thieves

Suggested incense: bayberry
Rob not the poor, because he is poor; Neither oppress the afflicted in the gate: For The Lord will plead their cause, And despoil of life those that despoil them. Proverbs 22:22

295. Prayer for Success from unfair competition

Prepare a red candle to repel.

The wrath of God came upon them, and slew the fattest of them, and smote down The chosen men of Israel. Psalms 78:31

296. Prayer to rise above any competition

Prepare a red candle to attract. A wise king scattereth the wicked, and bringeth the wheel over them. Proverbs 20:26

297. Prayer to Get better work from employees

Prepare a purple candle to attract.

Lord, my heart is not haughty, nor mine eyes lofty: neither do I exercise myself in Great matters, or in things too high for me. Psalms 131:1

298. Prayer to Rid yourself of troubles with money or business

Prepare a green candle to repel.

I will also make it a possession for the bittern, and pools of water: and I will sweep it with the besom of destruction, saith the LORD of hosts. Isaiah 14:23

299. Prayer For success in business

They shall be abundantly satisfied with the fatness of thy house; and thou shalt make them drink of the river of thy pleasures. Psalms 36:8

300. Prayer for Good fortune in business and money

Prepare a green candle to attract.

God is not man, that he should lie, or a son of man, that he should change his mind. Has he said, and will he not do it? Or has he spoken, and will he not fulfill it? Numbers 23:19

301. Prayer for the Rich and Poor: -

"Give us help from trouble, For the help of man is Useless." Psalms 60:11

302. Prayer for the Rich and Poor: -

"He raises the poor out of the dust, And lifts the Needy out of the ash heap," Psalms 113:7-8

303. Prayer for Economic Growth: -

"Then the earth shall yield her increase; God, our own God, shall Bless us." Psalms 67:6

304. Prayer Against Economic woes: -

"When they cast you down, and you say, 'Exaltation will Come!' Then He will save the humble person." Job 22:29

305. Prayer against Promise and Fail: -

„And the word of the LORD came to me, saying "Son of man, what is this proverb that you people have about the land Of Israel, which says, 'The days are prolonged, and every vision Fails'?"Tell them therefore, 'Thus says the Lord GOD: "I will lay this Proverb to rest, and they shall no more use it as a proverb in Israel." But say to them, "The days are at hand, and the fulfillment of every Vision." Ezekiel 12:21-23

306. Prayer for Success: -

"He shall be like a tree Planted by the rivers of water, That brings Forth its fruit in its season, Whose leaf also shall not wither; And Whatever he does shall prosper." Psalms 1:3

307. Prayer for Good Fortune: -

"Say to the righteous that it shall be well with them, For they shall eat The fruit of their doings." Isaiah 3:10

308. Prayer for Positive Planning:

"But the path of the just is like the shining sun, That shines ever Brighter unto the perfect day." Proverbs 4:18

309. Prayer Against Disappointments: -

"Be shattered, O you peoples, and be broken in pieces! Give ear, all You from far countries. Gird yourselves, but be broken in pieces; Gird Yourselves, but be broken in pieces. Take counsel together, but it will come to nothing; Speak the word, But it will not stand, For God is with us." Isaiah 8:9-10

310. Prayer Against Rise and Fall: -

"But the path of the just is like the shining sun, That shines ever Brighter unto the perfect day" Proverbs 4:18

311. Prayer for Wealth: -

"And you shall remember the LORD your God, for it is He who gives You power to get wealth, that He may establish His covenant which He swore to your fathers, as it is this day." Deuteronomy 8:18

312. Prayer Against Poverty: -

"I will make you a great nation; I will bless you And Make your name great; And you shall be a blessing." Genesis 12:2

313. Prayer to Recover Lost Blessings: -

"So I will restore to you the years that the swarming locust has eaten, The crawling locust, The consuming locust, And the chewing locust, My great army which I sent among you. You shall eat in plenty and be satisfied, And praise the name of the LORD your God, Who has dealt wondrously with you; And My people Shall never be put to shame." Joel 2:25-26

314. Prayer for Promotion: -

"For exaltation comes neither from the east Nor from the west nor From the south. But God is the Judge: He puts down one, And exalts another." Psalms 75:6-7

315. Prayer for Favor: -

"You love righteousness and hate wickedness; Therefore God, Your God, has anointed You With the oil of gladness more than Your Companions." Psalms 45:7

316. Prayer against blackmail by enemies:

"Be shattered, O you peoples, and be broken in pieces! Give ear, all You from far countries. Gird yourselves, but be broken in pieces; Gird Yourselves, but be broken in pieces. Take counsel together, but it will come to nothing; Speak the word, But it will not stand, For God is with us." - Isaiah 8:9-10

317. Prayer for Success in life's activities: -

"For You, O LORD, will bless the righteous; With favor You will

Surround him as with a shield". Psalms 5:12

318. Prayer for Employment: -

Let Your work appear to Your servants, And Your glory to their

Children. And let the beauty of the LORD our God be upon us, And establish The work of our hands for us; Yes, establish the work of our hands." Psalms 90:16-17

319. Prayer for Business opportunities: -

"I returned and saw under the sun that-The race is not to the swift, Nor the battle to the strong, Nor bread to the wise, Nor riches to men Of understanding, Nor favor to men of skill; But time and chance Happen to them all´. Ecclesiastes 9:11

Christian Good Luck in Wealth

320. Prayer To never have money worries again

Suggested incense: patchouli

Give no occasions of stumbling, either to Jews, or to Greeks, or to the church of God: even as I also please all men in all things, not seeking mine own profit, but the v profit' of the many, that they may be saved. 1st Corinthians 10:32-33

321. Prayer To get a raise

Suggested incense: peony

Servants, in all tilings do the orders of your natural masters; not only when their eyes are on you, as pleasers of men, but with all your heart, fearing the Lord: Whatever you do, do it readily, as to the Lord and not to men. Colossians 3:22-23

322. Prayer To attract customers

Prepare a green candle to attract.

And the multitudes gave heed with one accord unto the things that were spoken by Philip, when they heard, and saw the signs which he did. Acts 8:6

323. Prayer To get a better job

Prepare a green candle to attract.

For the Lamb which is in the midst of the throne shall feed them, and shall lead them unto living fountains of waters: and God shall wipe away all tears from their eyes. Revelation 7:17

324. Prayer for extra money

Charge them that are rich in this world, that they be not high minded, nor trust in uncertain riches, but in the living God, who giveth us richly all things to enjoy; That they do good, that they be rich in good works, ready to distribute, willing to communicate; Laying up in store for themselves a good foundation against the time to come, that they may lay hold on eternal life. 1 Timothy 6:17-19

325. Prayer for Breakthrough (Open doors): -

"For a great and effective door has opened to me, and there are Many adversaries." 1 Corinthians 16:9

326. Prayer for Divine Help/Wisdom: -

"for I will give you a mouth and wisdom which all your Adversaries will not be able to contradict or resist." Luke 21:15

327. Prayer against faulty foundation: -

"But He answered and said, "Every plant which my heavenly Father has not planted will be uprooted˙. Matthew 15:13

Muslim Good Luck in Wealth

328. Prayer to find a lost object

When an affliction befalls them, they say, "We belong to GOD, and to Him we are returning." Quran [2:156]

329. Prayer for Success in business

GOD has bought from the believers their lives and their money in exchange for Paradise. Thus, they fight in the cause of GOD, willing to kill and get killed. Such is His truthful pledge in the Torah, the Gospel, and the Quran - and who fulfills His pledge better than GOD? You shall rejoice in making such an exchange. This is the greatest triumph. Quran [9:111]

330. Prayer for Success in business

A. L. M. R.* These (letters) are proofs of this scripture. What is revealed to you from your Lord is the truth, but most people do not believe. - GOD is the One who raised the heavens without pillars that you can see, then assumed all authority. He committed the sun and the moon, each running (in its orbit) for a predetermined period. He controls all things, and explains the revelations, that you may attain certainty about meeting your Lord. - He is the One who constructed the earth and placed on it mountains and rivers. And from the different kinds of fruits, He made them into pairs - males and females. The night overtakes the day. These are solid proofs for people who think. Quran [13:1-3]

331. Prayer To increase sustenance

GOD is the One who created the heavens and the earth, and He sends down from the sky water to produce all kinds of fruit for your sustenance. He has committed the ships to serve you on the sea in accordance with His command. He has committed the rivers as well to serve you. - He has committed the sun and the moon in your service, continuously. He has committed the night and the day to serve you. - And He gives you all kinds of things that you implore Him for. If you count GOD's blessings, you can never encompass them. Indeed, the human being is transgressing, unappreciative. Quran [14:32-34]

332.   Prayer For abundance

GOD is fully aware of all His creatures; He provides for whomever He wills. He is the Powerful, the Almighty." Quran [42:19]

333.   Prayer For abundance

Anyone who trusts in GOD, He suffices him. GOD's commands are done. GOD has decreed for everything its fate." Quran [65:3]

334.   Prayer to remove poverty

1. Nun.   [These letters (Nun, etc.) are one of the miracles of the Qur'an, and none but Allah (Alone) knows their meanings].   By the pen and what the (angels) write (in the Records of men).   2. You (O Muhammad) are not, by the Grace of your Lord, a madman.   3. And verily, for you (O Muhammad) will be an endless reward.   4. And verily, you (O Muhammad) are on an exalted standard of character.   5. You will see, and they will see,   6. Which of you is afflicted with madness.   7. Verily, your Lord knows better, who (among men) has gone astray from His Path, and He knows better those who are guided.   8. So (O Muhammad) obey not the deniers [(of Islamic Monotheism those who belie the Verses of Allah), the Oneness of Allah, and the Messenger of Allah (Muhammad), etc.]   9. They wish that you should compromise (in religion out of courtesy) with them, so they (too) would compromise with you.   10. And obey not everyone who swears much, and is considered worthless,   11. A slanderer, going about with calumnies,   12. Hinderer of the good, transgressor, sinful,   13. Cruel, after all that base-born (of illegitimate

birth),   14. (He was so) because he had wealth and children.   15. When Our Verses (of the Qur'an) are recited to him, he says: "Tales of the men of old!"   16. We shall brand him over the nose!   17. Verily, We have tried them as We tried the people of the garden, when they swore to pluck the fruits of the (garden) in the morning,   18. Without saying: Insha'Allah (If Allah will).   19. Then there passed by on the (garden) something (fire) from your Lord at night and burnt it while they were asleep.   20. So the (garden) became black by the morning, like a pitch dark night (in complete ruins).   21. Then they called out one to another as soon as the morning broke,   22. Saying: "Go to your tilth in the morning, if you would pluck the fruits."   23. So they departed, conversing in secret low tones (saying), 24. No Miskin (poor man) shall enter upon you into it today. 25. And they went in the morning with strong intention, thinking that they have power (to prevent the poor taking anything of the fruits therefrom).   26. But when they saw the (garden), they said: "Verily, we have gone astray,"   27. (Then they said): "Nay! Indeed we are deprived of (the fruits)!"   28. The best among them said: "Did I not tell you: why do you not say: Insha' Allah (If Allah will)."   29. They said: "Glory to Our Lord! Verily, we have been Zalimun (wrong-doers, etc.)."   30. Then they turned, one against another, in blaming.   31. They said: "Woe to us! Verily, we were Taghun (transgressors and disobedient, etc.)   32. We hope that our Lord will give us in exchange a better (garden) than this. Truly, we turn to our Lord (wishing for good that He may forgive our sins, and reward us in the Hereafter)."   33. Such is the punishment (in this life), but truly, the punishment of the Hereafter is greater, if they but knew.   34. Verily, for the Muttaqun (pious and righteous persons) are Gardens of delight (Paradise) with their Lord. 35. Shall We then treat the (submitting) Muslims like the Mujrimun (criminals, polytheists and disbelievers, etc.)? 36. What is the matter with you? How judge you?   37. Or have you a Book through which you learn.   38. That you shall have all that you choose?   39. Or you have oaths from Us, reaching to the Day of Resurrection that yours will be what you judge. 40. Ask them, which of them will stand surety for that! 41. Or have they "partners"? Then let them bring their "partners" if they are truthful! 42. (Remember) the Day when the Shin shall be laid bare (i.e. the Day of Resurrection) and they shall be called to prostrate (to Allah), but they (hypocrites) shall not be able to do so, 43. Their eyes will be cast down, ignominy will cover them; they used to be called to prostrate (offer prayers), while they were healthy and good (in the life of the world, but they did not). 44. Then leave Me Alone with such as belie this Qur'an. We shall punish them gradually from directions they perceive not. 45. And I will grant them a respite. Verily, My Plan is strong. 46. Or is it that you (O Muhammad) ask them a wage, so that they are heavily burdened with debt? 47. Or that the Ghaib is in their hands, so that they can write it down? 48. So wait with patience for the Decision of your Lord, and be not like the Companion of the Fish, when he cried out (to Us) while he was in deep sorrow. (See the Qur'an, Verse 21:87). 49. Had not a Grace from his Lord reached him, he would indeed have been (left in the stomach of the fish, but We forgave him), so he was cast off on the naked shore, while he was to be blamed. 50. But his Lord chose him and made him of the righteous. 51. And verily, those who disbelieve would almost make you slip with their eyes through hatredness when they hear the Reminder (the Qur'an), and they say: "Verily, he (Muhammad) is a madman!" 52. But it is nothing else than a Reminder to all the 'Alamin (mankind, jinns and all that exists). Quran Chapter 68

335. Prayer to increase wealth

1. Al-Qari'ah (the striking Hour i.e. the Day of Resurrection),
2. What is the striking (Hour)? 3. And what will make you know what the striking (Hour) is? 4. It is a Day whereon

mankind will be like moths scattered about, 5. And the mountains will be like carded wool, 6. Then as for him whose balance (of good deeds) will be heavy, 7. He will live a pleasant life (in Paradise). 8. But as for him whose balance (of good deeds) will be light, 9. He will have his home in Hawiyah (pit, i.e. Hell). 10. And what will make you know what it is? 11. (It is) a hot blazing Fire!" Quran Chapter 101

336.   Prayer for Repayment of debts

Say, "Our god: possessor of all sovereignty. You grant sovereignty to whomever You choose, You remove sovereignty from whomever You choose. You grant dignity to whomever You choose, and commit to humiliation whomever You choose. In Your hand are all provisions. You are Omnipotent." Quran [3:26]

337.   Prayer for Wealth

"O Allah our Lord! Send us from heaven a table set (with viands), that there may be for us -for the first and the last of us - a solemn festival and a sign from You, and provide for our sustenance, for you are the best Sustainer (of our needs)". " (Quran: 5:114)

338.   Prayer For protection against thieves

The (Holy) Apostle believes in that (Book) which has been Sent down to him from his Lord; and so do the believers. Each one believes in all sincerity in Allah and His Angels and His Books and His Apostles; (and they proclaim): "We discriminate not against any of His Apostles." And they say: "We hear, and we obey. We seek Your Forgiveness, O our

Lord, and it is You to Whom we all are to return in the end." Allah does not burden any soul with more than it can bear. For it hall be the reward of what (good) it has earned, And against it shall be (the punishment of) What (evil) it has committed: "Our Lord! Call us not to account if we forget or err. Our Lord! Lay not on us such a (heavy) burden as You did lay on those who have passed away before us. Our Lord! Lay not on us that burden Which we have not the strength to bear. And pardon us; absolve us; and have mercy on us; You alone are our Friend and Helper; Help us to triumph over the unbelieving folk." Quran 2:285,286

339. Prayer for Blessings in business, farming, home, etc.

In the name of Allah, Most Beneficent, Most Merciful. Alif- Lam- Mim- Ra. These are the Verses of the Divine Book. And that which has been sent down to you from Your Lord is the Truth, but most of the people believe not (because of their wrong-headedness). Allah it is (the Mighty and the Wise) Who has raised The heavens without pillars (as) you see them, Then He settled (Himself) on the Throne of Power, And made the sun and the moon Subservient to His command. Each one running its course to an appointed term. He plans every affair, and explains clearly His Signs that haply You maybe certain of the Meeting with your Lord. And He it is Who has spread the earth, and Set therein firm mountains and rivers. And fruits of every kind He has made therein in pairs, Two and two. He covers the day with the night. Verily in all these are Signs of His Might For a people who reflect." Quran 13:1,3

340. Prayer for blessings in produce, livestock, etc

Allah is He Who has created the heavens and the earth And sends down water (rain) from the sky, And thereby brought forth fruits as provision for you; And He has made the ships to be of service to you, That they may sail through the sea by His Command; And He has made rivers (also) to be of service to you. And He has made the sun and the moon, Both constantly pursuing their courses, To be of service to you; and He has made the night and the day, to be of service To you. And He gave you of all that you asked for, And if you count the Blessings of Allah, Never will you be able to count them. Verily! Man is indeed an extreme Wrong-doer, a disbeliever." Quran 14:32,34

341. Prayer For abundance in fortune

Allah is gracious unto His servants. He provides for whom He wills. And He is the Strong, the Mighty." Quran 42:19

342. Prayer For abundance in fortune

And whoever puts his trust in Allah, He will suffice him. Lo! Allah brings His commands to pass. Allah has set a measure for all things." Quran 65:3

343. Prayer for Repayment of debts

Say: O Allah! Master of the sovereignty! You give sovereignty to whomever You desire, And withdraw sovereignty from whomever You desire. You exalt whomever You desire and debase whomever You desire.

In Your hand is goodness. Truly, You possess power over everything." Quran 3:26

Good Luck Charms in Wealth

344. A Horn

The horn, signifies strength power and abundance. Sometimes called the horn of plenty, this charm signifies future wealth and prosperity.

Like crescents, which they resemble, charms in the form of animal horns are believed to have great power over the evil eye.

345. A Circle

The circle is one of mankind's oldest symbols of good fortune. It stands for eternity because it is without beginning or end. It is a sign of completeness, perfection, and wholeness.

The concept gave us many kinds of lucky symbols, including rings of every description and the circular designs of Amish hex signs, not to mention the wreaths we hang on our doors at Christmas-time.

346. An Axe

Axes are lucky charms that can bring success. Archaeologists have unearthed talismans in the shape of an Axe head in all parts of the world. They usually have holes in them, indicating that they were worn around the neck.

Ancient art from the Far East, pre-Columbian America, the Mediterranean, and Africa frequently depicts a double-bladed Axe to indicate power.

347.   Coins

"See a penny pick it up and all day long you'll have good luck. Leave it there and you'll despair."

Some even take the idea of luck to the other side of the coin, and believe that if the coin is face down that it's best to leave it on the ground. Luckiest of all, are Coins that are bent or have holes in them, especially if they turn up as change after making a purchase. The luck of such Coins is enhanced if they are carried in a left-hand pocket or worn around the neck.

Coins can bring luck in many ways. - You will have good luck if you keep a jar of pennies in the kitchen. - The first Coin you receive each day should be placed in an otherwise empty pocket and it will attract more.

- A Coin in a new jacket, handbag, or wallet will bring good luck. - If you get pennies as change on a Monday, you will have good luck all week long. - Many people consider it lucky to carry a Coin with their birth date.

- Some say that a Coin minted in a leap year will bring good fortune.

Coins also have a place in Feng Shui, as luck bringers.

348. Frogs

The Frog has been a symbol of prosperity, wealth, friendship and abundance in many cultures and a symbol of fertility in others.

In the Native American culture of the Southwest, the Frog carries a piece of wood in its mouth, because the Mojave people believe Frogs brought fire to humans.

For the Romans, the Frog was a mascot believed to bring Good Luck to one's home.

The native Aborigines of Australia, believed that Frogs brought the thunder and rain, to help the plants to grow.

Frogs are also said to be effective in speeding up recovery from disease.

349. Tigers

Tigers are considered lucky in Chinese astrology.

The Tiger is also considered a protector against certain evils, including theft and fire.

350. Rainbows

Rainbows are considered lucky, because we all know, if we find the end of the Rainbow, there will be a pot of gold.

351. Alfalfa:

Carried in a mojo hand for money luck.

352. Alkanet Root Bark:
To prevent jealous losers from jinxing you or your winnings.

353. Alligator Tooth:
An old Southern charm; fragile, but powerful to renew money.

354. Allspice Berries:
Carried in a mojo hand for money luck.

355. Bayberry Root:
Carried in a mojo hand for money luck.

356. Chamomile Hand Wash:
Tea made from golden flowers cleans the hands for money.

357. Cinnamon Chips:
Carried in a mojo hand for money luck.

358. Four-Leaf Clover:
Pressed flat in the wallet to draw money, health, luck, and love.

359. Horseshoe:

Hung over the door for protection and luck to all who dwell within.

360. John the Conquer Root:

Carried in the pocket for good luck in money and love.

361. Lodestone:

Magnetic iron ore use to "draw" money, luck, or whatever is desired.

362. Pyrite:

Sparkling golden iron ore that attracts money to it; carried in the pocket.

363. Rabbit Foot:

The ultimate down-home Southern amulet, for fortune carried as a key ring charm.

364. Silver Dime:

Protection against conjure and assurance of luck in money matters.

365. Money Incense

1 part basil
1 part cinquefoil
1/2 part hyssop

1/2 part galangal

366. Orange candles
- General success
- Property deals
- Legal matters
- Justice
- Selling

367. Crystals
shaped like ingots, Green, purple And red crystals as well as stones such as raw emeralds, raw Rubies, garnets, carnelians, amethysts, iolite, jet, mica, agate, Amber, tiger eye and jade attract money into your life.

368. Zircon
Energizes the body and will; heightens awareness and sharpens the intellect; brings rich rewards; overcomes obstacles or opposition; strengthens the constitution; safe guards travellers and property.

369. Chalcedony
attracts public favor, recognition And financial reward; increases popularity, Enthusiasm and fitness; dispels gloom, Despondency, envy or anger; affords protection To travellers and helps nursing mothers

370. Onyx

looks after business shrewdness; vitalizes The imagination and increases stamina; dispels Nightmares and eases tension; brings emotional And mental relief.

371. Almandine

is linked with achievement, Improvement, self-confidence and Determination. It enhances psychic ability; Makes clear existing problems or difficulties; Overcomes rivalry and obstacles in the form of Human behavior

372. Cat's eye

encourages success in speculative Ventures or competitive sport; strengthens ties of Love or affection; protects the home from danger;

373. Blue John

attracts honors, wealth, prestige And social success; improves business and Personal relationships; guards the wearer Against injury or accident while travelling; Mitigates the envy of others.

374. Alunite

attracts good fortune, health and Happiness; helps understanding and domestic Harmony; speeds recovery from illness; protects Home and property against physical and Psychic danger.

Manifest Good Luck in Wealth

375. Manifest goals

close your Eyes and visualize the goals as if it's already achieved. You have to emit a new signal with your thoughts, and those Thoughts should be that you currently have more than enough.

The shortcut to anything you want in your life is to BE and FEEL happy now! It is the Fastest way to bring money and anything else you want into your

Focus on radiating out into the Universe those feelings of joy And happiness. When you do that, you will attract back to you all Things that bring you joy and happiness

376. Manifest money

You have got to feel good about money to attract more to you. Understandably when people do not have enough money they do not Feel good about money, because they don't have enough. But those Negative feelings about money are stopping more money coming To you! You have got to stop the cycle, and you stop it by starting to Feel good about money, and being grateful for what you have. Start To say and feel, "I have more than enough." "There is an abundance

Of money and it's on its way to me." "I am a money magnet." "I Love money and money loves me." "I am receiving money every Day." "Thank you. Thank you. Thank you'

Good Luck in Happiness

Chinese Good Luck in Happiness

377. Feng shui to increase happiness

To increase your prosperity you would Enhance the Southwestern wall or corner with red lights (fire) Next to a jade plant (wood) next to a bowl of coins (metal) next To an aquarium filled with goldfish or a picture depicting Goldfish.

378. Feng shui to increase happiness

The colors purple, red and green, These three colors support Prosperity energy in a space. A pleasant still life to attract this Energy is a pretty glass bowl containing a purple amethyst, a Red carnelian and a green piece of jade.

379. Feng shui to increase happiness

The Jade plant is the ultimate symbol of Prosperity for the Chinese. It's flat round leaves and compact Shape makes it the Asian equivalent of a money tree.

380. Feng shui that prevents happiness

Dead or withering plants: Anything obviously decomposing is Antithetical to the energy of prosperity and should be Removed

381. Feng shui that prevents happiness

Trash cans. Like the toilet, this item drains vital energy from The prosperity

382. Feng shui that prevents happiness

Images of Poverty or Want: Art that depicts objects or Landscapes in a withering, rustic or decomposing state should Not be displayed. Also avoid placing photographs of Yourself when you were going through a "broke phase" here. You might repeat the situation!

Wiccan Good Luck in Happiness

383. Spell For More Energy

I breathe in brightness, life and power
I breathe out sadness, tired, old,
With every breath I draw within me
Living energies unfold
From my tingling toes
Through my legs it flows
To my body, to my heart
To my head, that is a start
Flowing freely all through me
Bright and glorious energy
Make me light and make me free
Tis my will, so shall it be!

The time has come
To let my body rest
And gently, I drift
Away

Away
From the day
And into the night
Starlit bright,
The color blessed dimensions
Are awaiting me.

There I will do
My work and my play
Until it is time
To return to the day

Smooth and gentle
Ocean wide,
In and out
In even Flow -

Now I bid myself goodnight
And with that,
Turn out the light.

384.　　Spell for "drawing out" curses and hexes from your energy

use a salt medicine pouch, worn over the heart (the heart of energy in the center of the chest, between the nipples, not the flesh heart).

The heart of energy always tries to get rid of "rubbish" that collects in our wider energy system; it is going to push from its end so you get a powerful conjunction that gets rid of the curses or hexes powerfully and reliably.

Get a piece of wax paper or another kind of strong paper. Write on it carefully what you know about the curses/hexes, like who cast them, or where they came from, and/or when this started (the date). If you don't know any details, just write "My two curses or hexes" on the paper so that we all know what this for and what it's going to do.

Place three spoonfuls of salt (rock salt, or sea salt, or just ordinary table salt) into the paper and make a bundle out of it that you can tie to a piece of string.

Wear it over your heart for three days and three nights. The salt will draw out the curses or hexes and take them into itself. On the morning of the fourth day, open the package, and let water wash the salt away. You can do this in a river or by an ocean shore, scatter it outside when it is raining hard, or simply in your sink if you have no access to flowing water elsewhere. Burn the paper and the string.

Jewish Good Luck in Happiness

385. Prayer to turn bad luck into good

Suggested incense: cinquefoil

And said, naked came I out of my mother's womb, and naked shall I return thither: the Lord gave, and the Lord hath taken away; blessed be the name of the Lord Job 1;21

386. Prayer To receive guidance

Suggested incense: vanilla

For I know the plans I have for you, says the Lord. They are plans for good and not for evil, to give you a future and a hope. Jeremiah 29:11

387. Prayer For good luck and happiness

Suggested incense: honeysuckle

I will give thanks unto thee; for I am fearfully and wonderfully made: Wonderful are thy works; And that my soul knoweth right well. Psalms 139:14

388. Prayer To receive instructions in dreams

Suggested incense: lavender
Then surely you could lift up your face without spot; Yes, you could be steadfast, and not fear; Because you would forget *your* misery, And remember *it* as waters *that have* passed away, And *your* life would be brighter than noonday.
Though you were dark, you would be like the morning." Job 11:15-17

389. Prayer to remove any curse

Suggested incense: pine

And I will bring the blind by a way that they know not; in paths that they know not will I lead them; I will make darkness light before Them, and crooked places straight. These things will I do, and I will not forsake them." Isaiah 42:16

390. Prayer To appreciate life to its fullest

Suggested incense: rose

There is nothing better for a man than that he should eat and drink, and make his soul enjoy good in his labor. This also I saw, that it is from the hand of God." Ecclesiastes 2:24

391. Prayer To be free of unclean thoughts and deeds

Suggested incense: lavender

Depart ye, they cried unto them, Unclean! Depart, depart, touch not! When they fled away and wandered, men said among the nations, They shall no more sojourn "here*. Lamentations 4:15

392. Prayer To find inner strength

Suggested incense: rosemary Fear ye not me? Saith The Lord: will ye not tremble at my presence, who have placed the sand for the bound of the sea, by a perpetual decree, that it cannot pass it? And though the waves thereof toss themselves, yet can they not prevail; though they roar," Jeremiah 5:22

393. Prayer To know the truth

Suggested incense: honeysuckle And if thou sell aught unto thy neighbor, or buy of thy neighbor's hand, ye shall not wrong one another." Leviticus 25:14

394. Prayer to Cleanse the spirit

Suggested incense: lotus
He alone spreads out the heavens, And treads on the waves of the sea; He made the Bear, Orion, and the Pleiades, And the chambers of the south; He does great

things past finding out, Yes, wonders without number. Job 9:8-10

395. Prayer To turn sadness into joy

Suggested incense: frankincense

The works of the Lord are great, Studied by all who have pleasure in them, His work is honorable and glorious, And His righteousness endures forever, He has made His wonderful works to be remembered; The LORD is gracious and full of compassion" Psalms 111:2-4

396. Prayer To dispel fear

Prepare a purple candle to repel.

He mocketh at fear, and is not affrighted; neither turneth he back from the sword. Job 39:22

397. Prayer To bring joy and happiness to your family

Prepare a green candle to attract.

I said to myself, "Look, I have increased in wisdom more than anyone who has ruled over Jerusalem before me; I have experienced much of wisdom and knowledge.". Ecclesiastes 1:16

398. Prayer To gain prospective in the face of difficulty

Prepare a blue candle to attract.

Now therefore, our God, the great, the might}', and the terrible God, who keepest covenant and loving kindness, let not all the travail seem little before thee, that hath come upon us, on our kings, on our Princes, and on our priests, and on our prophets, and on our fathers, and on all thy people, since the time of the kings of Assyria unto this day". Nehemiah 9:32

399. Prayer for Protection from malevolent spirits

"From on high he sent fire; into my bones he made it descend; he spread a net for my feet; he turned me back; he has left me stunned,   faint all the day long." Lamentations 1:13

400. Prayer To have a night of pleasant dreams

Prepare a white candle to attract.

And I will lay thy flesh upon the mountains, and fill the valleys with thy height. Ezekiel 32:5

401. Prayer Stop your boss from bothering you

Prepare a purple candle to repel.

Yet will I leave a remnant, that ye may have some that shall escape the sword among the nations, when ye shall be scattered through the countries. Ezekiel 6:8

402. Prayer To receive an answer to a question

Prepare a blue candle to attract.

Woe is me! For I am as when they have gathered the summer fruits, as the grape gleanings of the vintage: there is no cluster to eat: my soul desired the First ripe fruit. Micah 7:1

403. Prayer to Remove bad luck and all curses

Prepare a white candle to repel.

Nevertheless they were disobedient, and rebelled against thee, and cast thy law behind their backs, and slew thy prophets which testified against them to turn them to thee, and they wrought great provocations. Nehemiah 9:26

404. Prayer To lose your troubles

Prepare a blue candle to repel.

And Pharaoh said unto him, Get thee from me, take heed to thyself, see my face no more; for in that day thou seest my face thou shalt die. Exodus 10:28

405. Prayer to gain spiritual power

Prepare a purple candle to attract.

And they did bind the breastplate by his rings unto the rings of the ephod with a lace of blue, that it might be above the curious girdle of the ephod, and that the breastplate might not be loosed from the ephod; as the Lord commanded Moses. - Exodus 39:21

406. Prayer Make good wishes come true

Prepare a red candle to attract.

Many, O LORD my God, are Your wonderful works Which You have done; And Your thoughts toward us Cannot be recounted to You in Order; If I would declare and speak of them, They are more than can be numbered. Psalms 40:5

407. Prayer for the Good upbringing of Little Children: -

"Here am I and the children whom the LORD has given me! We are For signs and wonders in Israel From the LORD of hosts, Who dwells In Mount Zion." Isaiah 8:18

408. Prayer for Courage and Patience: -

"Only be strong and very courageous, that you may observe to do According to all the law which Moses My servant commanded you; do Not turn from it to the right hand or to the left, that you may prosper Wherever you go." Joshua 1:7

409. Prayer Against War: -

"Violence shall no longer be heard in your land, Neither wasting nor Destruction within your borders; But you shall call your walls Salvation, And your gates Praise." Isaiah 60:18

410. Prayer Against foul spirits/evil yoke: -

"It shall come to pass in that day That his burden will be taken away From your shoulder, And his yoke from your neck, And the yoke will Be destroyed because of the anointing oil." Isaiah 10:27

411. Prayer for Continuous Growth and Up-liftment: -

"But the path of the just is like the shining sun, That Shines ever brighter unto the perfect day." Proverbs 4:18

412. Prayer for Continuous Growth and Upliftment: -

"But my horn You have exalted like a wild ox; I have Been anointed with fresh oil." Psalms 92:10

413. Prayer Against Devilish Plans/water spirits:

"No weapon formed against you shall prosper, And Every tongue which rises against you in judgment You shall condemn. This is the heritage of the servants of the LORD, And their Righteousness is from Me," Says the LORD." Isaiah 54:17

414. Prayer Against Devilish Plans/water spirits:

"For there is no sorcery against Jacob, Nor any Divination against Israel. It now must be said of Jacob And of Israel, 'Oh, what God has done!' Numbers 23:23

415. Prayer for Peace, Oneness and Unity: -,

"For unto us a Child is born, Unto us a Son is given; And The government will be upon His shoulder. And His name will be Called Wonderful, Counselor, Mighty God, Everlasting Father, Prince Of Peace." Isaiah 9:6

416. Prayer for Peace, Oneness and Unity: -,

"LORD, You will establish peace for us, For You have Also done all our works in us." Isaiah 26:12

417. Prayer Against Evil Initiations: -

"No weapon formed against you shall prosper, And every tongue Which rises against you in judgment You shall condemn. This is the heritage of the servants of the LORD, And their righteousness is from Me," Says the LORD." Isaiah 54:17

418. Prayer Against witches and wizards: -

"A man or a woman who is a medium, or who has familiar spirits, Shall surely be put to death; they shall stone them with stones. Their Blood shall be upon them." Exodus 22:18

419. Prayer Against Monitoring spirits: -

"O you who dwell by many waters, Abundant in treasures, Your end Has come, The measure of your covetousness." Jeremiah 51:13

420. Prayer Against Occult Covenant:

"No weapon formed against you shall prosper, And every tongue Which rises against you in judgment You shall condemn. This is the Heritage of the servants of the LORD, And their righteousness is from Me," Says the LORD." - Isaiah 54:17

421.   Prayer Against Evil curses: -

"Like a flitting sparrow, like a flying swallow, So a curse without Cause shall not alight." Proverbs 26:2

Christian Good Luck in Happiness

422.   Prayer To banish evil spirits

Suggested incense: violet

Put on the whole armor of God, that ye may be able to stand against the wiles of the devil. Ephesians 6:11

423.   Prayer To increase psychic powers

Suggested incense: cinnamon

For if the word spoken through angels proved steadfast, and every transgression and disobedience received a just recompense of reward; how shall We escape, if we neglect so great a salvation? Which having at the first been spoken through the Lord, was confirmed unto us by them that heard; God also bearing witness with them, both by signs and wonders, and by manifold powers, and by gifts of the Holy Spirit, according to his own will." Hebrews 2:2-4

424.   Prayer Calm a troubled youth

Suggested incense: passionflower

These things command and teach. Let no man despise thy youth; but be thou an ensample to them that believe, in word, in manner of life, in love, in faith, in purity. Till I come, give heed to reading, to exhortation, to teaching. 1st Timothy 4:11-13

425. Prayer to Contact your spirit guide

Prepare a purple candle to attract.

Whom I have sent unto you for the same purpose, that ye might know our affairs, and that he might comfort your hearts." Ephesians 6:22

426. Prayer To rid yourself of bad dreams

Prepare a white candle to repel.

And those that weep, as though they wept not; and those that rejoice, as though they rejoiced not; and those that buy, as though they possessed not; 1 Corinthians 7:30

427. Prayer For wisdom and knowledge

Every valley shall be filled, and every mountain and hill shall be brought low; and the crooked shall be made straight, and the rough ways shall be made smooth. Luke 3:5

428. Prayer to Rid home of troublesome spirits

Prepare white candle to repel.

And that which thou sowest, thou sowest not that body that shall be, but bare grain, it may chance of wheat, or of some other grain. 1 Corinthians 15:37

429. Prayer to Cleanse a home from negative energy

Prepare a white candle to repel.

That it might be fulfilled which was spoken by the prophet, saying, I will open my mouth in parables; I will utter things which have been kept secret from the foundation of the world. Matthew 13:35

430. Prayer to Help a friend who is depressed

Prepare a blue candle to attract.

Do not love the world or the things in the world. If anyone loves the world, the love of the Father is not in him. For all that is in the world—the desires of the flesh and the desires of the eyes and pride in possessions—is not from the Father but is from the world. And the world is passing away along with its desires, but whoever does the will of God abides forever. 1 John 2:15-17

431. Prayer To remove the evil eye

Prepare a white candle to repel.

And it is God who establishes us with you in Christ, and has anointed us, and who has also put his seal on us and given us his Spirit in our hearts as a guarantee. 2 Corinthians 1:21-22

432. Prayer to Remove a curse

Prepare a purple candle to repel.

Now to the King eternal, immortal, invisible, to God who alone is wise, be honor and glory forever and ever, Amen. 1 Timothy 1:17

433. Prayer for good luck

"We know that in everything God works for good with those who love him, who are called according to his purpose." (Romans 8:28)

434. Prayer to Control Anger: -

"And do not be conformed to this world, but be transformed by the Renewing of your mind, that you may prove what is that good and Acceptable and perfect will of God" Romans 12:2

435. Prayer for good behavior: -

"That ye may be blameless and harmless, the sons of God, without Rebuke, in the midst of a crooked and perverse nation, among whom Ye shine as lights in the world;" Philippians 2:15

436. Prayer Against Agents and rulers of darkness: -

"For we do not wrestle against flesh and blood, but against Principalities, against powers, against the rulers of the darkness of This age, against spiritual hosts of wickedness in the heavenly Places." Ephesians 6:12

437. Prayer against Occult Serpent: -

"You are of God, little children, and have overcome them, because He who is in you is greater than he who is in the world." 1 John 4:4

438. Prayer to Overcome the Devil:

"For whatever is born of God overcomes the world. And This is the victory that has overcome the world--our faith." 1 John 5:4

439.   Prayer to Overcome the Devil:

"And they overcame him by the blood of the Lamb And by the word of their testimony, and they did not love their lives to The death." Revelation 12:11

440.   Prayer to defeat my enemies: -

"But bring here those enemies of mine, who did not want me to reign Over them, and slay them before me.'" Luke 19:27

441.   Prayer for Continuous Growth and Upliftment: -

"Humble yourselves therefore under the mighty hand of God, that he may exalt you in due time:" 1 Peter 5:6

442.   Prayer for Religious Harmony: -

"There is one body and one Spirit, just as you were called in   one Hope of your calling; One Lord, one faith, one baptism; One God and Father of all, who is above all, and through all, and in You all." Ephesians 4:4-6

443.   Prayer for Peace, Oneness and Unity:

"Now I am no longer in the world, but these are in the World, and I come to You. Holy Father, keep through Your name Those whom You have given Me, that they may be one as We are." John 17:11

444. Prayer to cast out evil spirits: -

"And these signs will follow those who believe: In My name they will Cast out demons; they will speak with new tongues;" Mark 16:17

445. Prayer against Ancestral demons: -

"But Jesus rebuked him, saying, "Be quiet, and come out of him!" And When the demon had thrown him in their midst, it came out of him and Did not hurt him". Luke 4:35

446. Prayer against forces of darkness: -

"For we do not wrestle against flesh and blood, but against Principalities, against powers, against the rulers of the darkness of This age, against spiritual hosts of wickedness in the heavenly Places". Ephesians 6:12

Muslim Good Luck in Happiness

447. Prayer for renewal of faith

Our Lord, we believe in what You have sent down, and we follow the apostle, so write us among the witnesses. " Quran (3:53)

448. Prayer to strengthen your faith

Our Lord! Do not make our hearts swerve after You have guided us, and bestow Your mercy on us. Indeed You are the All-Bountiful" Quran .(3:8)

449.   Prayer for melancholy and depression

"To make strong your hearts and to keep your feet firm thereby." Quran [8:17]

450.   Prayer For melancholy and depression

They are the ones whose hearts rejoice in remembering GOD. Absolutely, by remembering GOD, the hearts rejoice" Quran [13:28]

451.   Prayer for Curing someone who is under the influence of evil

"Did you think that we created you in vain; that you were not to be returned to us?" - Most exalted is GOD, the true Sovereign. There is no other god beside Him; the Most Honorable Lord, possessor of all authority. - Anyone who idolizes beside GOD any other god, and without any kind of proof, his reckoning rests with his Lord. The disbelievers never succeed. - Say, "My Lord, shower us with forgiveness and mercy. Of all the merciful ones, You are the Most Merciful." Quran [23:115-118]

452.   Prayer for Curing someone who is under the influence of evil

"Allah is He besides Whom there is no god, the Ever living, the Self-subsisting by Whom all subsist; slumber does not overtake Him nor sleep; whatever is in the heavens and whatever is in the earth is His; who is he that can intercede with Him but by His permission? He knows what is before them and what is behind them, and they cannot comprehend anything out of His knowledge except what He pleases, His knowledge extends over the heavens and the earth, and the preservation of them both tires Him not, and He is the Most High, the Great. There is no compulsion in religion; truly the right way has become clearly distinct from error; therefore, whoever disbelieves in the Shaitan and believes in Allah he indeed has laid hold on the firmest handle, which shall not break off, and Allah is Hearing, Knowing. Allah is the guardian of those who believe. He brings them out of the darkness into the light; and (as to) those who disbelieve, their guardians are Shaitans who take them out of the light into the darkness; they are the inmates of the fire, in it they shall abide." Quran 2:255-257

453. Prayer for curing someone who is under the influence of evil

"Say (O Muhammad): "It has been revealed to me that a group (from three to ten in number) of jinns listened (to this Qur'an). They said: 'Verily! We have heard a wonderful Recital (this Qur'an)! It guides to the Right Path, and we have believed therein, and we shall never join (in worship) anything with our Lord (Allah).'And exalted be the Majesty of our Lord, He has taken neither a wife, nor a son (or offspring or children). 'And that the foolish among us [i.e. Iblis (Satan) or the polytheists amongst the jinns] used to utter against Allah that which was wrong and not right. 'And verily, we thought that men and jinns would not utter a lie against Allah." Quran 72:1-5

454. Prayer To remove fear and fright

"When you read the Quran, we place between you and those who do not believe in the Hereafter an invisible barrier. - We place shields around their minds, to prevent them from understanding it, and deafness in their ears. And when you preach your Lord, using the Quran alone, they run away in aversion." Quran [17:45-46]

455. Prayer for Removing fear

"GOD is the best Protector, and, of all the merciful ones, He is the Most Merciful." Quran [12:64]

456. Prayer for Protection against evil men and jinn

"Say: "I seek refuge with (Allah) the Lord of the daybreak, "From the evil of what He has created; "And from the evil of the darkening (night) as it comes with its darkness; (or the moon as it sets or goes away)."And from the evil of the witchcrafts when they blow in the knots, "And from the evil of the envier when he envies." Quran Chapter 113

457. Prayer for protection against evil men and jinn

"In the name of Allah, the Most Beneficent, the Most Merciful. Say: I seek refuge in the Lord of mankind, The King of mankind, The God of mankind, From the evil of the sneaking whisperer, Who whispereth in the hearts of mankind, Of the jinn and of mankind." Quran Chapter 114

458. Prayer for being In Distress

Say: "O my Lord! judge Thou in truth!" "Our Lord Most Gracious is the One Whose assistance should be sought against the blasphemies you utter!" (Quran: 21:112)

459. Prayer for being In Distress

"Allah is Sufficient for us, and He is the Best Disposer of affairs". (Quran: 3:173)

460. Prayer for being In Distress

Who say, when afflicted with calamity: "To Allah We belong, and to Him is our return". (Quran: 2:156)

461. Prayer for being In Distress

"Our Lord! bestow on us Mercy from Yourself, and dispose of our affair for us in the right way!" (Quran: 18:10)

462. Prayer for being in Distress

"Our Lord! remove the Penalty from us, for we do really believe!" (Quran: 44:12)

463. Prayer for being In Distress

"But Allah is the best to take care (of them), and He is the Most Merciful of those who show mercy!" (Quran: 12:64)

464. Prayer for being In Distress

"O My Lord! Truly am I in (desperate) need of any good that You bestow on me!" (Quran: 28:24)

465. Prayer for being In Distress

"There is no god but You: Glorified are You: Truly I have been of the wrongdoers!" (Quran: 21:87)

466. Prayer for Protection from Satan

And say "O my Lord! I seek refuge with You from the whisperings (suggestions) of the Shayatin (devils) "And I seek refuge with You, My Lord! lest they should come near me." (Quran: 23:97)

467. Prayer for release from imprisonment

Our Lord, take us out of this town whose people are oppressors And raise for us from yourself one who will protect us And raise for us from yourself one who will help us." Quran 4:75

468. Prayer for Nightmares

For them are glad tidings in the life of this World and the hereafter. There is no change in the word of Allah. This is, without doubt, supreme felicity." Quran 10: 64

469. Prayer For melancholy and depression

"To make strong you hearts and to Keep your feet firm thereby." Quran 8:17

470. Prayer For melancholy and depression

Who have believed and whose hearts are at ease In the remembrance of Allah. Verily in the remembrance of Allah do hearts find rest." Quran 13:28

471. Prayer For lessening one's burden

Now has Allah lightened Your burden for He knows that there is weakness in you. So if there be of you, a hundred steadfast, they shall Overcome two hundred and if there be of you a thousand They shall overcome two thousand by the permission of Allah. And Allah is with the steadfast." Quran 8:66

472. Prayer for Curing someone under the influence of evil

Do you think We have created you in jest And that you would not be brought back to Us (for accountability)? Hence, exalted be Allah, The True King. None is worthy of worship besides He, The Lord of The Throne of Honour." Quran 23:115,118

473. Prayer for Curing someone under the influence of evil

In the Name of Allah, the Most Beneficent, the Most Merciful. All the praises and thanks be to Allah, the Lord of the 'Alamin (mankind, jinns and all that exists). The Most Beneficent, the Most Merciful. The Only Owner (and the Only Ruling Judge) of the Day of Recompense (i.e. the Day of Resurrection) You (Alone) we worship, and You (Alone) we ask for help (for each and everything).Guide us to the Straight Way The Way of those on whom You have bestowed Your Grace, not (the way) of those who earned Your Anger, nor of those who went astray Quran Chapter 1

474. Prayer to remove fear and fright

And (O My Apostle!) When you recite the Quran, We set up (to intervene) between you and those Who believe not in the Hereafter a hidden Veil invisible to the eye And We put coverings on their Hearts that they may not understand it, And (cause) a heaviness in their ears. And when you mention your Lord alone in the Quran, They flee away turning on their back in aversion (from the Truth) Quran 17:45,46

475. Prayer for removing fear

And Allah is the best of Protectors and He is The Most Merciful of all who show Mercy. Quran 12:64

476. Prayer To halt an oppressor from oppressing

And you will remember what I say unto you. confide my cause unto Allah. Lo! Allah is ever watchful over his slaves. " Quran 40:44

Prayer for Removing of a calamity

Allah suffices for us and He is the Best Disposer of affairs." Quran 3:173

477. Prayer for divine help when trying to prove one's innocence.

He said: O my Lord! Help me against their calling me a liar"
Quran (23:26)

478. Prayer for gratitude

My Lord! Inspire me to give thanks for Your blessing with which You have blessed me and my parents, and that I may do righteous deeds which may please You, and admit me, by Your mercy, among Your righteous servants."
Quran (27:19)

Good Luck Charms for Happiness

479. Hand

In just about every Mediterranean country, charms in the shape of human hands have been powerful symbols of good luck.

In Muslim countries, the hand is made with the thumb and fingers outstretched in honor of Fatima, the favorite daughter of the prophet Mohammad.

480. Cat's Eye

The Cat's Eye clears all obstacles and helps one to move ahead in life. It also wards off the Evil Eye, Ghosts, Spirits and negative planetary influences.

In India, it is common wisdom that if one carries a cat's-eye stone, fortune will never diminish. Among gamblers, it is a charm of choice to bring luck in games of chance.

It protects one from unforeseen losses in business or profession, and ensures financial stability, by guarding the owner's wealth.

481.   Amber

Amber is thought to be a bit of the sun with the power to bring good fortune.

The Greeks called this Amber "elektron", which gave us our word of electricity, and its power to give off sparks when rubbed may be why many people have considered it a lucky charm. Both the Chinese and the Muslims burn amber as incense as a protection against evil spirits.

482.   Nautical Star

The Nautical Star, or North Star, is seen as providing guidance, and it is a good luck symbol for sailors.

The Star of Bethlehem guided the three wise men; in the Old Testament, the starry sky symbolized the numerous children of Abraham, and gave direction to the promised land.

483.   Horseshoe

A Horseshoe symbolizes good luck, keep evil away, good fortune and fertility.

Horseshoes have associations with the strength and dependability of the horse, and, in an upright position, it is also symbolic of the moon. Pointing downwards, it is symbolic of the womb. To the Greeks, it symbolized the crescent moon which was regarded as a symbol of fertility.

The Horseshoe protects one's house and land, to keep strangers away, when hung up on the wall of a home or above a doorway. The "U" shape will hold good luck inside forever.

484. Red Chinese Lanterns

These Lanterns are a symbol of happiness and good luck in the Chinese culture.

485. Dream Catchers

Dream catchers, from Native American culture, are considered good luck, because they catch the negative images from dreams.

486. Red Bats

In China, Red Bats are symbols of long life, and amulets are worn as lucky charms to bring happiness.

The red bat is thought to ward of evil. Five red bats can also represent the "five good fortunes" of health, longevity, love, wealth and virtue.

487. Eggs

In England, a gift of a white Egg is considered lucky, but a brown Egg, not only brings luck, but happiness as well.

488.   Ladybugs

The Ladybug is considered a harbinger of good luck and prosperity. It shall free you from day to day problems. Wearing a Ladybug amulet or having a live one land on you will brighten your day, give you patience with those around you, and most importantly, lessen your burdens.

Killing a Ladybug is considered bad luck.

If one lands on you when you are ill, it takes any illness away.

If a Ladybug lands on your hand and then flies away, it said to be good weather on the following Sunday.

Spots: If a Ladybug lands on the hand of a recently married woman, the number of dots on its back, is the number of children she will have. The number of spots on a Ladybug can also indicate the number of happy months that are ahead. And, folklore also suggests, if you catch a Ladybug in your home, count the number of spots, that's how many dollars you'll soon find.

489.   Dragonflies

Dragonflies are another lucky insect.

As a creature of the wind, the dragonfly represents change. As a creature of the water, they represent the subconscious, or "dream" state.

Other symbolic meanings associated with dragonflies, are prosperity, strength, courage, peace, harmony and purity.

490. Scarabs

Scarabs date back to Ancient Egypt, when Scarabs were considered good luck beetles.

As a symbol of the rising sun and a protector from evil; the Scarab, is also a symbol of rebirth, regeneration and transformation.

491. Improve Luck Incense

1 part rosemary
1/2 part dragon's blood resin
1/2 part musk root
1/2 part sandalwood
Few drops of rose oil
Few drops of musk oil

492. Ending Negativity Incense

1 part marjoram
1 part thyme
1/2 part oregano
1/4 part bay leaves
1/4 part cloves

493. Banishing evil Incense

1 part bay leaves
2 parts cinnamon
1 part rose petals
2 parts myrrh resin
Pinch of salt

494. Jinx-removing Incense

2 parts clove

1 part deers tongue

Few drops of rose geranium oil

495. Exorcism Incense

3 parts frankincense resin

1 part rosemary

1 part bay leaves

1 part avens

1 part mugwort

1 part St John's Wort

1 part angelica

1 part basil

496. Luck:

Apple, ash (leaves), hazel, holly (for Newly-weds), ivy (for newly-weds), mint, rose, Rowan, vervain, violet (flowers)

497. Happiness:

Anise, catnip, lily of the valley, Marjoram, saffron Harmony: Hyacinth, heliotrope, lilac, Meadowsweet

498. Blue candle

• The Element of Water

- Wisdom
- Protection
- Calm
- Good fortune
- Opening
Communication
- Spiritual inspiration

499.   Aventurine

Promotes health, vigor and cheerfulness; it promises emotional moral support in new commercial undertakings; gets rid of doubt, diminishes anxiety and eases bodily aches and pains; strengthens resolve against hardship.

500.   Zircon

energizes the body and will; heightens Awareness and sharpens the intellect; brings rich Rewards; overcomes obstacles or opposition; Strengthens the constitution; safeguards Travellers and property.

501.   Gypsum

signifies hope and youthfulness, and Benefits children and adults wanting to 'go it Alone'. It reduces swellings and aids digestion; Averts the envy of others; and brings peace of Mind.

502.   Pumice

is linked with purity, vision, truth and Development. It helps sociability and personal Gain; bestows success on long-term ventures; Guards against illusion and delusion; brings Comfort to a troubled mind or spirit.

503. Rock crystal

represents purity, hope and Chastity; expands conscious awareness and Prophetic visions; brings trust and harmony; Dispels bad dreams, delusion and illusion; Safeguards the very young and astral travellers From harm.

504. Chrysoprase

brings joy to the wearer; sharpens The intellect, opens up new areas and rewards Initiative; gets rid of envy, jealousy and Complacency; dispels anxiety, lifts depression And helps insomnia.

505. Aquamarine

encourages hope, and promotes Youthfulness and physical fitness. It is a Powerful token of love and friendship; eases Digestive or nervous disorders and mental Distress; renews confidence and energy; relaxes Fear.

506. Coral

helps vitality, good humor and Harmonious relationships; expands horizons And helps encourage development; prevents Damage to crops and property; protects Travellers, mariners and small children.

507. Carnelian

helps with peace, pleasure and Prosperity; brings joy to those going on a long Journey or moving house; offers protection to Travellers, speakers and expectant mothers; Assuages strife, anger and disappointment.

Manifest Good Luck in Happiness

508.   Manifest your happiness

• A shortcut to manifesting your happiness is meditate on what your true happiness would be and then see your desires as an Absolute fact in your life. Believe what makes you happy is in your life and then you will sooner or later see the doors for your true happiness open for you.

Your power is in your thoughts, so stay aware. In other words, "Remember to remember." That your thoughts are the energy opening or closing the door to your happiness.

509.   Exercise the happiness

While the door to your true happiness is opening, do things in the mean time that strengthen your "happy energy". Do the things that you love and that bring you joy to stay in the frame of mind of happiness. This includes being around happy people and happy places.

It is important that the happiness is not derived from a substance such as drugs or alcohol because that is sadness in disguise, covering a pain that is truly dissolved by natural happiness. Drugs or alcohol expand your sadness by creating legal, financial, or physical damage whereas a natural happiness such as exercise will surely help improve your life.

Conclusion

Philosophy of Good Luck

"And when affliction touches man, he calls upon God, whether lying on his side or sitting or standing; but when We remove from him his affliction, he continues [in disobedience] as if he had never called upon God to [remove] an affliction that touched him. Thus is made pleasing to the transgressors that which they have been doing" (Qur'an: 10:12)

"And when We bestow Our Grace on man (the disbeliever), he turns away and becomes arrogant (far away from the Right Path). And when evil touches him, he is in great despair." (Qur'an: 17:83)

"When trouble touches men, they cry to their Lord, turning back to Him in repentance: but when He gives them a taste of Mercy as from Himself, behold, some of them pay part-worship to other god's besides their Lord (Qur'an: 30:33)

The philosophy of good luck is to stay apprecative, to stay grateful in good times and bad. Stay optimistic and follow the good teachings of those blessed with guidance.

The second philosophy of good luck is to be open to good teachings. I am a Muslim and I follow Islam because after researching and practicing many religions, I am comfortable with and believe in the teachings of Islam. Islam also teaches that many Prophets came before Prophet Muhammad and taught beautiful teachings as well. Therefore, sayings of Abraham, Moses, Buddha and Jesus are equally blessing.

To benefit from past and present teachers is our duty and benefits us, for example, we benefit every day from the use of electricity taught to us by Thomas Edison, that does not make us bad people or heathens for using a source of power discovered by Edison, ultimately the source of power is a gift from God and using it and thanking God for it is our duty.

The most tranquil people I have met in my travels are those who are one with God, regardless of their economic or social status, because they are in a state of mind of appreciating their Creator, then they are happy to be alive.

In conclusion, exercise your spiritual, mental, emotional, and physical health. See the cup as half full instead of half empty. For example, half the world sees the number 13 as bad luck and the other half see it as good luck, so focus your energy on seeing the number 13 as good luck! See good luck in everything you do and everything that is done too you and enjoy life!

The Gospel is also called "Good News", the Christians have taken the lead in the mass media campaign, broadcasting radio and video shows to share with the world their "good news". In this same fashion, "Good Luck Radio" GoodLuckRadio.com and "Good Luck Videos" GoodLuckVideos.com have been created to broadcast 24/7 positive prayers, verses, mantras, chants and spells from various beliefs around world to bring good energy to your life. Spotlighting the heart of the Holy books' written formulas that are widely accepted by their billions of followers to bring good fortune.

Like lightening, good energy is abundant, thus we can all appreciate and share each other's formulas for getting Good Luck, so as most religions teach: "Help Thy Neighbor" and recommend the scientific formulas in this book to others and listen to GoodLuckRadio.com and watch GoodLuckVideos.com to help you and your loved ones get Good Luck!

Bibliography

Abdullah, Yusuf Ali. *The Holy Qur'an, English Translation of the Meanings and Commentary.* Madinah, Saudi Arabia: King Fahd Holy Qur'an Printing Complex, 1991.

The Bible, King James Version. Oak Harbor, WA: Logos Research Systems, Inc., 1995.

The Good News Translation. Grand Rapids, MI: Zondervan, 2001.

26 Secrets of Feng Shui" Palm Springs, California , Aquarian Publications, 2002
,
Remedies from the Quran, Pakistan, Darul Ishaat Publishing, 1994

White Spells, Woodbury Minnesota, Llewellyn Publications, 2001

Bible Spells, New Brunswick NJ, Inner Light Publications, 2007

Jesus Christ Prayer Manual, River State Nigeria, Club of Christ International, 2010

Luck Factor, Auckland New Zealand, Arrow Books, 2004

Principles of Manifesting, London UK, Dream Manifesto, 2011

Luck: The Essential Guide, NYC, NY, William Borrows Publishing, 2008

The Good Luck Book: An A-to-Z Guide to Charms and Symbols, Gramercy, Louisiana, Gramercy Books, 1999

The Secret, NYC, NY, Atria Books, 2006

The Ultimate book of spells, London UK, Arcturus Publishing, 2007